JOYCE BAILEY ANDERSON,
SHEILA DUBMAN & ALEXANDRA FIANDACA

PRINCETON
MASSACHUSETTS

A HISTORY OF ITS VILLAGES

Charleston   London

THE
History
PRESS

Published by The History Press
Charleston, SC 29403
www.historypress.net

First published 2009

Manufactured in the United States

ISBN 978.1.59629.631.2

Library of Congress Cataloging-in-Publication Data

Anderson, Joyce Bailey.
Princeton : a history of its villages / Joyce Bailey Anderson, Sheila Dubman and
Alexandra Fiandaca.
p. cm.
Includes bibliographical references.
ISBN 978-1-59629-631-2
Princeton (Mass. : Town)--History. 2. Wachusett Mountain (Mass.)--History. I. Dubman,
Sheila. II. Fiandaca, Alexandra. III. Title.
F74.P9A527 2009
974.4'3--dc22
2009012245

This book is dedicated to the late Dennis Rindone, Princeton's town administrator, who was taken from us in 2009. His warmth, enthusiasm and devotion to Princeton will never be forgotten. His support of the Princeton Historical Commission is, in great part, responsible for this book.

CONTENTS

CONTENTS

PREFACE

The history of Princeton, Massachusetts, is still being written. In the past few years, the Princeton Historical Commission has successfully nominated four districts for inclusion in the National Register of Historic Places.

Historic districts are carefully defined geographic areas, designated as historic by virtue of a concentration of historically significant buildings. This book is a celebration of Princeton's historic districts and the historic structures that qualify them as special. It focuses on the physical artifacts that previous generations have left behind. By observing, describing and seeking to understand these artifacts, we have come to understand the history they reveal and the people who created them.

ACKNOWLEDGEMENTS

This book is a celebration of Princeton's inclusion in the National Register of Historic Places. It is based on work presented in the National Register nominations written by Kathryn Cavanaugh, Susan Ceccacci and Anne Forbes. We thank them all for their excellent work.

We also owe thanks to the Princeton Historical Society for the use of many of the photographs in this book, the staff at the Princeton Public Library for their assistance, Harvey Schmidt for his title-searching expertise and Phil Mighdoll for his technical and editorial support.

This book is a project of the Princeton Historical Commission and we are grateful to our tireless members. We thank the residents and the Town of Princeton for loans of material and for their generous support.

We are grateful to the Massachusetts Historical Commission for encouraging our efforts and acknowledging these districts.

The cover of the book was taken from a painting done in 1991 by Vern Hall, a former Princeton resident. The title is *Croquet on Princeton Common, circa 1875*.

Finally, we are thankful to the National Park Service for the national recognition that these districts have brought to Princeton.

CHAPTER ONE

A VERY BRIEF HISTORY OF PRINCETON

FIRST, THERE WAS A MOUNTAIN

It is impossible to come to Princeton and miss Wachusett Mountain. In 1632, John Winthrop, first governor of the Massachusetts Bay Colony, traveled to "Boston Rock" in what is now the city of Waltham. He recorded a remarkable sight in his journal: "A very high hill due west about forty miles off." At that time, neither the governor nor any of the colonists knew the name of that "hill" to be Wachusett or had any understanding of the area's terrain. Within just a few years, Governor Winthrop and his people laid out the Bay Path from Boston to the Connecticut Valley and points west. This path followed native trails and crossed right through Princeton.

At over two thousand feet above sea level, Wachusett is the highest point in Massachusetts east of the Connecticut River. It is a natural focal point in Princeton and has been for longer than anyone can remember. The native peoples recognized Wachusett as a ceremonial site and a landmark useful for hunting and staging during King Philip's War.

Our more recent ancestors took a less reverent interest in the mountain. In 1825, Mrs. John P. Rice became the first European to reach the top of the mountain on horseback, eclipsing Phineas Gregory's earlier achievement with a team of oxen. In the same year, there was an attempt to change the name to Mount Adams in honor of the new president, John Quincy Adams. Adams's admirers promoted this name change with a celebration on the summit, flashy enough to be seen from Boston. In spite of the bells, parades, cannon fire and bonfire, the name change was never adopted.

A view of Wachusett Mountain from Sunset Rock, where the first meetinghouse was located. *Princeton Historical Society.*

Princeton Center nestled at the foot of Wachusett Mountain, as seen from the east. *Princeton Historical Society.*

A Very Brief History of Princeton

Princeton has attracted tourism since the first surveyors climbed to the top of the mountain in 1830. Currently, more than 600,000 people visit the mountain every year, some to ski and some to enjoy the magnificent views.

Wachusett Mountain became a symbol of Victorian American culture when Thoreau wrote "A Walk to Wachusett" and called Wachusett the "observatory of the state." By the 1870s, the Summit House hotel was built for the comfort of summer hikers and then expanded to include a dance pavilion for a more formal crowd. In 1900, Massachusetts established the Wachusett Mountain State Reservation.

Although Princeton "shares" the mountain with an adjacent town, there is no disputing the fact that the mountain is the heart and soul of Princeton. All who live in or visit Princeton know the sense of joy when they catch a glimpse of the mountain. Today's residents are prone to referring to Wachusett as "my mountain," expressing its importance to our sense of place.

THEN, THERE WAS A TOWN

With a centerpiece like Wachusett Mountain, Princeton's table has always been set for a historical banquet. Princeton has a lot of history on which to build. After Governor Winthrop and his people laid out the Bay Path right through Princeton, it still took nearly a century for the region to be settled by colonists. The earliest colonial settlers found this part of central Massachusetts to be a dangerous, inhospitable frontier, rocky and unsuitable for agriculture. The area that is now Princeton was part of the territory that was purchased from the Naguag tribe in 1686 and established as Rutland in 1713.

The region was beset by frequent wars between the colonists and the indigenous tribes until the end of Queen Anne's War in 1713. That marked the end of a prolonged period of warfare that thwarted early attempts at settlement. The colonists' perception that this land was dangerous did not die so easily and development was slow. The colonists were right to be wary. Hostilities were renewed with a vengeance during King Philip's War. By 1723, nearly all of the settlers in the nearby town of Rutland had left in fear of an imminent attack. That attack did occur in August of that year, and the provincial government proved unable to offer adequate protection to any of the settlements around Rutland. This period of warfare continued until a peace treaty was signed in 1725. This time around the peace held, but the perception that the land was worthless persisted.

Permanent settlement began in earnest in the 1730s because the General Court of Massachusetts was eager to expand beyond the borders of the Bay Colony in order to develop new sources of tax revenue. To that end, there was a great deal of surveying activity in this period and many large grants of land were made. For his services in laying out plans of the East Wing of Rutland, the Reverend Mr. Thomas Prince was granted sixty-three acres and an additional seventy-two "very Rocky" acres "in consideration of great care & labour he has taken in calculating & Computing ye Divisions above mentioned & other good services perform'd to the proprietors."

This was not the Reverend Mr. Prince's first piece of Princeton property, but to understand his importance to the town we should understand a bit about who he was. The Reverend Mr. Thomas Prince was born in Sandwich, Massachusetts, and graduated from Harvard College in 1707. After ten years of travel and preaching, he returned to Boston in 1717 and ascended to the pulpit of the Old South Church in 1718. He continued to preach there for the rest of his life. He was considered, along with his more famous colleague Cotton Mather, to be one of the most learned men in New England and directed much of his considerable intellect to the study of history. It was said, during his lifetime, that "nothing came from his pen that does not now possess historical value. His occasional papers are all luminous with the spirit and life of the time."

He purchased his first piece of land, over thirteen hundred acres in the township of Rutland, in 1727. By the end of his life, he is believed to have accumulated a total of about three thousand acres.

Although Mr. Prince lived in Boston and not in the town that bears his name, he probably traveled there frequently. A trip that now takes an hour would have taken him three days and involved stops with several friends in more settled areas along the way. The last several miles of his journey would have been on rough roads with no comforting sights of houses or inns by the wayside.

By the 1740s and '50s, a few more settlers arrived in the East Wing of Rutland and built homesteads while the French and Indian War was raging. In 1759, the district was reestablished as "Prince Town" in honor of the Reverend Thomas Prince, the largest landowner at that time. The building of a meetinghouse put Prince Town "on the map" as an independent community in 1763–64, when the colonist population was 284. Formal incorporation of Prince Town followed in 1771, by which time the population had soared to 701.

Before the Revolutionary War, Princeton was considered a poor agricultural community. By the end of the eighteenth century, logging,

THOMAS PRINCE A.M.

Quintus Ecclesiæ Australis Bostoni Novangloram Pastor, è Collegii Harvardini

The Reverend Mr. Thomas Prince (1687–1758), largest early landowner in Princeton and benefactor to the town. *Princeton Historical Society.*

milling and some manufacturing had been added to the economic mix and Princeton was seen as prosperous. Over the years, the town has gone through a number of changes, but Princeton has remained as strikingly beautiful as the site that Governor Winthrop saw in 1632.

CHAPTER TWO

LET'S GO DOWNTOWN

The Princeton Center Story

Princeton Center is often described as idyllic for good reason. It retains its charming, "frozen in time" appearance as the center of local government, with gracious private homes, the oldest building dating to 1765, gathered around a pristine town common. Princeton Center has not succumbed to the commercialization or heavy traffic that has forever changed many other New England town centers.

The town common still serves as a gathering place and focal point for community activities. It is also a visual backdrop for the public buildings set high above the common.

What is not so apparent is that the "center" of the town of Princeton was not always where it is now. By the late 1750s, Princeton had about twenty-five homesteads that were widely scattered within its boundaries. Princeton's first "town center" was located in Russell Corner, where Lieutenant Abijah Moore hosted a small group of men and women in his home and tavern. Then it was established about a half mile north on both sides of Mountain Road. Its "migration" was gradual and understandable.

The Princeton Center story began around 1761, when land was donated for a meetinghouse on what became known as Meeting House Hill. The early period ended when a new meetinghouse was built in the area that is now the town common. The late period began in 1937, when the last of the major summer houses for wealthy residents was built.

This early period of Princeton Center began once the residents of the newly created Prince Town finished debating the site for their new meetinghouse for dual use as a place for local government and for worship. They settled on a five-acre hilltop site donated by John and Caleb Mirick on the east side of Mountain Road. Abijah Moore was paid about sixty-six pounds to frame the building in late 1761, and construction was completed in 1763. The beginning of road construction accompanied this building activity, starting in 1762, connecting the new meetinghouse on Mountain Road to Sterling and Worcester Roads. The roads around the original Princeton Center date back much further than any structures. Mountain Road, for example, goes back to the seventeenth century, when the first European investors in the area gradually widened and improved the original footpath that was used by the Nipmuck tribe.

In spite of the lack of finished floors, windows and doors, the building hosted its first meeting in 1763. In 1764, church services were held, and the building was finally finished, complete with plastering and painting, in 1770. Since the meetinghouse served a dual purpose as church and public meeting spot, the first true town center developed around it on Meeting House Hill. This first meetinghouse was replaced near its original site in 1796. Its replacement remained standing until about 1838, although it was known, by this time, as the Congregational Church.

Moses Gill donated twenty acres directly across Mountain Road (on the west side) to be used as a town common and burial ground. The burial ground, now known as Meeting House Cemetery, was established in 1765. Moses Gill was Princeton's wealthiest citizen during the early days of Princeton Center. In addition to his long career as a Boston merchant, his prosperity can be credited to his marriage to Sarah Prince, daughter of Thomas Prince and sole heir to his landholdings. Later in his life, Gill was instrumental in the success of the American Revolution and became lieutenant governor of Massachusetts. Years after Sarah's death, he inherited the vast Prince estate and married Rebecca Boylston, the aunt of Ward Nicholas Boylston. In what is either an ironic twist or a remarkable example of continuity, Mr. Boylston played an important role in reestablishing Princeton Center at its present location, just a few decades after his uncle Moses Gill established it on Meeting House Hill.

Meeting House Cemetery, on Mountain Road at the intersection of Allen Hill Road, is the remaining heart of the early Princeton Center. Built in 1765, it is surrounded by dry-laid stone walls and is the final resting place of many of Princeton's early settlers and their descendants. A stroll through Meeting House Cemetery is an introduction to prominent names in Princeton's history, including Mirick, Howe, Russell, Moore, Brooks, Cheever and Merriam.

Moses Gill is not buried here, but some of his family members are here, along with three of Gill's "Negro servants," who may, in fact, have been slaves. Perhaps most poignant among the many graves of young children are the six Harrington family children who all died during one month in

Meeting House Cemetery, the final resting place of many of Princeton's early settlers. *Joyce Anderson.*

the winter of 1786, along with a hapless young woman who happened to be visiting the family.

There are three tombs at the south edge of the cemetery, outside of the wall, in an area that looks like a grassy mound. The names of those in these tombs are marked on the outside face of the cemetery wall, an unusual feature. Many of the older headstones feature arched tops, angelic images of human faces and feathered wings or urns surrounded by weeping willows. The earliest headstones are dated 1770 and the latest, 1897. (The last burial was actually in the 1930s.) Since the meetinghouse was relocated to the present Princeton Center in 1838, only about thirty-four more individuals were buried there after 1850.

Meeting House Cemetery was soon joined, in 1768, by the adjacent town pound. Town pounds were built to house stray livestock, an important function in the eighteenth century. Princeton's first pound was located in a barn on Caleb Mirick's farm on Merriam Road and was moved to this site in 1768 on land donated by Moses Gill. This typical enclosure of dry-laid stone walls was once heightened with a wood fence that has long since disappeared.

By 1774, the cemetery and pound had another neighbor. The original Centre School, also known as Schoolhouse No. 1, was the first "official" schoolhouse built in Princeton. Before that time, school was conducted in the homes of the schoolmasters. The Centre School burned down in 1788 and a second schoolhouse was built on the same site in 1792.

The cemetery, the pound and the roads are the only surviving structures of this early town center. There were no commercial businesses at this site, likely because it was hard to get there in the winter. In Puritan New England, missing a Sabbath meeting was a serious offense and, in some cases, even resulted in imprisonment. Having a town's only meetinghouse on top of a hill in a region prone to snow and ice presented an intolerable situation for those who lived on farms in the lowlands in the southern part of town.

The next phase of development saw the town center moved to a more convenient central location, at its present site south of the meetinghouse, near a store, tavern and blacksmith shop. By 1810, Princeton had grown large enough that the Centre School district was divided in half. The old 1792 schoolhouse was closed and two new schools were built in other locations. In 1816, the old Centre School building was converted into the first Princeton Town Hall, separate from the church, and probably served that purpose until 1842, when Boylston Hall was built in the new town center area.

While Princeton showed itself to be ahead of its time by separating town business from religious influence in 1816, the rest of the commonwealth did not adopt a constitutional amendment separating church and state until 1833 and continued to operate in the older fashion of combining religious services and town business under the same roof. This radical action in Princeton resulted from differences of opinion within the church about the selection of a new pastor. The town fathers intervened, and their involvement was met with resistance from the church: "We cannot consent to give up our rights and privileges, and sanction the irregularity of receiving a minister in whose call and settlement we have not a primary and distinct voice." The town then "resolved to proceed independent of the church."

The current Princeton Center emerged as the new heart of town from 1819 to 1847. Thirteen properties, including the town common, the Congregational Church, the Boylston Burial Ground and the Wachusett House Annex, date to that period. By 1830, all of the roads presently in the district (except for Allen Hill Road and Town Hall Drive) had been laid out.

In the first half of the nineteenth century, Princeton's cattle population was twice as high as its human population. In the 1820s, some manufacturing activity was added to Princeton's agricultural economy. The big change for

The earliest known photograph of Princeton Common at a time when the church and its horse sheds were located at the head of the common. *Princeton Historical Society.*

Princeton, however, came when stagecoaches, and later railroads, started bringing tourists to Princeton. The development of a summer tourist industry brought changes to Princeton that would last until automobiles made distant vacation destinations accessible to more people.

Some of the most familiar buildings in Princeton, including the present town hall, library and the Princeton Center School, were built between 1883 and 1906, during the heyday of summer tourism. By then, Princeton was a popular summer resort, offering a clean, spring-fed oasis from city life. The building boom near the town common encouraged wealthy people to build large summer homes with fantastic views of Wachusett Mountain. At the same time, inexpensive Bungalow-style houses were built for the less affluent who were eager to enjoy Princeton's summer climate.

While new construction was going on, several older buildings were "modernized." Many houses were updated with mansard roofs, bay windows and porches, fashionable choices at the time. Four buildings were moved from their original sites to other nearby sites within the district. The Wachusett House Tavern was built in 1822 and moved to 7 Boylston Avenue

Prospect House, later known as the Princeton Inn, was located on the east side of the common. It was a popular hotel in the heyday of summer tourism. It was the last hotel to burn in 1923. *Princeton Historical Society.*

in 1847. The Reverend Samuel Clarke House was built in 1819 and moved to 10 Mountain Road in 1838. The Congregational Church, built in 1838, was moved to 14 Mountain Road in 1884. The Stratton-West House, built as Centre School No. 1 on top of Meeting House Hill in 1789, is believed to have been moved to 19 Hubbardston Road in 1834.

The district has lost just two historic properties since 1937 and only eight new structures have been added. The Princeton Center Historic District is a remarkably intact historical treasure. Princeton became a quieter rural town again after the last of the resort hotels burned down in 1923. Only three primary structures were built between 1928 and 1937. Princeton Center is now one of the loveliest, best-preserved examples of what people all over the world love about New England towns.

The Princeton Center Historic District was listed in the National Register of Historic Places on February 26, 1999, by the National Park Service. It consists of three publicly owned properties on eleven acres of land in the heart of Princeton: the town common, Bagg Hall (the town hall) and the Goodnow Memorial Building (the public library).

The Princeton Center Historic District was expanded on March 10, 2006. The expanded district includes the old Meeting House Hill area, as well as the previously listed Princeton Center area. It includes 165 acres, with forty-six buildings and sites, twenty-three barns and other outbuildings. We can

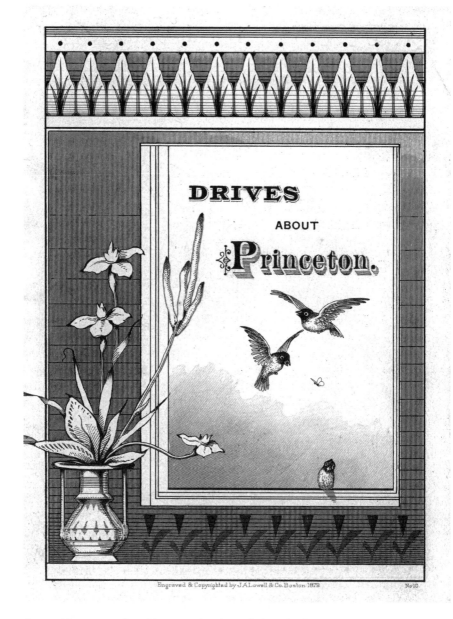

A pamphlet encouraging visitors to enjoy the varied scenic "Drives About Princeton."
Princeton Historical Society.

still see an exhilarating range of architectural styles in the Princeton Center Historic District, including Colonial, Federal, Greek Revival, Italianate, Second Empire, Shingle, Queen Anne, Richardsonian Romanesque, Colonial Revival and Craftsman Bungalow. This variety is a testament to the changing means and aspirations, as well as tastes, of our ancestors. Princeton Center is not a time capsule of one particular era but a record of changing times. It is and was home to individuals who expressed the tastes of their times within the means of their own circumstances. Most of the buildings are made of wood and sited close to the street and to one another. These historic properties are a fine illustration of the story of Princeton Center, progressing from an eighteenth-century agricultural community, through its glory days as a summer resort around the turn of the twentieth century to its current status as the hub of a beautiful New England town.

AN UNCOMMON COMMON STORY

If you stand on the town common, you see an uncommon display of historic buildings and a broad sweep of local history. You will see Princeton's finest public buildings, as well as many private homes that were built for that purpose. Other homes have more diverse stories to tell. Some look very much as they did when they were built, while others have been modified to reflect the changing styles of the times, making them more challenging to classify. These changes in fashion are still visible in their bay windows, mansard roofs, porches and more. Here are some of their stories.

Princeton's town common has been maintained as open space since at least the late 1830s. A small group of commercial enterprises had formed at the southern end as early as the late eighteenth century. It appears that a donation of land to the town in 1818 by Ward Nicholas Boylston allowed this piece of land to be set aside as a common, near the sites of the future church and town house. To make room for the new church, the Reverend Samuel Clarke's house was moved across the street. The new church was itself later moved, in 1884, to open up an unobstructed view of the newer Goodnow Memorial Building and to accommodate construction of the present Bagg Hall.

As in other New England towns, establishment of a common parcel of land would have seemed natural to people accustomed to grazing livestock and drilling local militias. Town commons have served many purposes over the years and remain magnets for social and civic activities. Princeton's town common now appears as a triangular public park bounded by Mountain

An early picture of Bagg Hall standing alone in all of its glory. Town meetings, high school graduations and other town events were held here. *Princeton Historical Society.*

Road, Hubbardston Road and Town Hall Drive. The basic size and shape of the town common has remained essentially unchanged since the 1830s.

The two stately public buildings that define the Princeton Center were built at roughly the same time but in very different styles. Both buildings express the tastes and expansive optimism of their time and both are due to the generosity of one individual, Edward Goodnow, a descendant of one of Princeton's founding families.

Edward Augustus Goodnow, born in 1810, started his career in Princeton. He was a talented entrepreneur, manufacturer and wholesaler. In 1866, he became president of the First National Bank of Worcester. Mr. Goodnow's considerable talents were put to many good uses, including leadership in the abolitionist movement, support of the Union in the Civil War and bequests to many institutions of higher learning. He lived to the age of ninety-six.

Bagg Hall, also known as Princeton Town Hall, was built in 1884–85 to replace the previous town hall. Known as Boylston Hall, this older building was on the east side of Mountain Road and burned down in 1883. The new Bagg Hall was designed by architect Stephen C. Earle, who also designed

The stenciling and the chandelier evoke a sense of grandeur in the interior of the second floor of Bagg Hall. *Princeton Historical Society.*

the library next door. Earle studied architecture under Calvert Vaux, a well-known New York architect. Based in Worcester, he designed many public and private buildings in Massachusetts.

When the Goodnow Memorial Building (also known as the Princeton Public Library) had just been completed in 1883, Edward Goodnow offered a matching grant to the town to build a new town hall. He also offered to move the church to its present site to make space for the new town hall. Edward Goodnow donated money for construction and asked that the building be named Bagg Hall to honor his deceased first and second wives. They were sisters whose maiden name was Bagg.

Bagg Hall is a two-story Victorian Gothic/Romanesque Revival building. The foundation is made of granite and the walls are of pressed red brick trimmed with Longmeadow, Massachusetts brownstone. The roof is dark Maine slate with a louvered ventilation cupola on top. The recessed center entrance is set inside a deep stone portico under a brownstone arch. The most notable feature is a seventy-eight-foot-tall cylindrical turret, with a steeply pitched conical slate roof to the left of the main entrance. The building is further graced by red terra cotta and brick corbelling under the cornice. Many of the original interior finishes survive to this day. This building is a wonderful example of the late Victorian taste for gothic grandeur and a testament to the enthusiastic optimism of the town.

The Goodnow Memorial Building was designed in 1882 to house both a public library and a school. The school occupied the west side, with a separate entrance. The library section, under the clock tower, was on the east side of the building. The building was donated to the town by Edward Goodnow and dedicated to the memory of his wives, Harriet Goodnow and Mary Augusta Goodnow, and his son, Henry Bagg Goodnow. In 1906, having outgrown its space, schooling was moved to the site of the present Princeton Center building (18 Boylston Avenue). The library grew to occupy the entire Goodnow Memorial Building.

This building is a fine example of Richardsonian Romanesque style and is truly a New England treasure. It has a local granite foundation; walls are made of rough-faced Milford, Massachusetts granite and the trim of Longmeadow, Massachusetts brownstone. The roof is made of dark Maine slate. The seventy-foot-tall clock tower houses a Howard clock with a bell inscribed with the words "Goodnow Memorial Building, Knowledge is Power." Many beautiful decorative features that typify its era still grace the

A view of the stately Goodnow Memorial Building with the P.C. Doolittle House in the background. *Princeton Historical Society.*

library today. It, too, expressed the optimistic vision of a town that wished to declare that it "had arrived!"

The Congregational church is a direct descendant of the original Puritan church/meetinghouse that is so central to the history of most New England towns. This building was constructed in 1838 at the north end of the town common. In 1884, the building was moved across the road to its current location at 14 Mountain Road to make way for the construction of Bagg Hall. It is the third meetinghouse to be used by the Congregational Church in Princeton.

The wood-frame, Greek Revival building is two stories tall with a raised granite and brick foundation. The steeple contains an 1815 Paul Revere bell salvaged from the second meetinghouse. The steeple was rebuilt after the devastating 1938 hurricane that left much of New England in ruins. The church features another relic salvaged from the first meetinghouse: a small oculus window in the pediment, with the date 1762 in its center. There are more historic treasures inside, including a crystal and brass chandelier donated by a descendant of Ward Nicholas Boylston, and a Cole Organ Co. organ, installed in 1904 and paid for, in part, by the generous Mr. Edward Goodnow.

A view of Prospect Street looking west toward the Congregational Church. *Princeton Historical Society*.

The Princeton Center School, featuring its original separate boys' and girls' entrances. *Princeton Historical Society*.

Although not visible from the common, the former Princeton Center School on Boylston Avenue is another one of "downtown" Princeton's treasures. In 1906, the town built the Center School to accommodate a growing student population. It had, at first, seventy-four students in grades one through twelve. By the mid-1950s, students in grades nine through twelve began attending a regional high school in Holden. The Princeton Center School was used in this period to educate seventh and eighth graders. Now closed as a school, the building still serves the town as the Princeton Community Center by housing various civic and cultural activities.

This wood and stone, Shingle-style school with arched gothic windows, separated by pilasters with Ionic caps, is typical of schools of its era. A two-story, wood-shingled addition was built on the rear of the building in 1937 to accommodate a growing school population. The horse barn that stood to the right of the school is no longer there. Other changes were made in the last century to express changes in society. The school's two sets of identical doorways were originally used as separate entries for boys and girls. The left-hand entry was altered in the mid-1990s by extending the doorway forward to accommodate a handicap-accessible bathroom inside the building.

Directly across the road from the town common, on Hubbardston Road, is the Boylston Burial Ground, a final resting place for the Boylston family.

The Princeton Center School, class of 1916, posing at the school. *Princeton Historical Society.*

Mr. Boylston died in 1828 and his mausoleum was built on this site. His wife, Alicia, and all of his immediate family members are buried in the tomb. In 1870, his grandson, Dr. Ward Nicholas Boylston, gave the town an endowment for the perpetual maintenance of the burial ground. The last family member to be interred here died in 1893.

The elaborately decorative, cast-iron gate set in the stone wall surrounding the burial ground leads to a gentle slope. Out of view from the road, the mausoleum is made of granite blocks, topped with a distinctive stone urn, carved to appear to be draped with cloth. Its granite door has a decorative wrought-iron gate and is inscribed with the names of ten Boylston family members.

Ward Nicholas Boylston (1747–1828) became a summer resident of Princeton in 1804 and acquired extensive lands. In 1818, he donated land on the east side of Mountain Road for the construction of a new town house. His gift, Boylston Hall, was finally built in 1842. That building burned down in 1883 and was replaced by Bagg Hall.

Most of the historic buildings visible from the town common are private homes. That fact alone makes Princeton's common most uncommon, indeed. Here are some of their stories.

The building known as Wachusett House Tavern was originally known as "Wachusett House" and was also known as "the Annex" and "Wachusett Cottage." It was built by John Brooks Sr. in 1822 and was moved to its present site at 7 Boylston Avenue around 1847. The building may have been used as a private residence until the late nineteenth century, when the owner of the second Wachusett House hotel, Phineas Beaman, purchased and remodeled it as a twenty-room annex to the hotel next door. Originally built in the vernacular Federal style, this building has three stories with a distinctive mansard roof and pedimented dormers. The mansard roof was added sometime between 1877 and 1883, as was the three-story addition at the rear.

The Princeton House File shows that the Josiah D. and Richard Gregory House at 12 Boylston Avenue may be the third house built on this site. The first was built before 1897 and burned later that year. A second house was built in 1898 by John Mayley, who probably also built the existing barn. This second house burned in 1900. In 1904 Josiah D. Gregory bought the land and built the house we see here now. Richard Gregory, Josiah's son, owned the house from 1913 to 1917. The Gregory family operated the D.H. Gregory & Co. Store from 1840 to 1942. The two-story Dutch Colonial–style house has a granite foundation, wood shingling and an enclosed sleeping porch on the second floor.

The John Mayley Barn at 12 Boylston Avenue was built, not surprisingly, by John Mayley, who also built the second house on this site. This side-gabled barn was constructed sometime between 1871 and 1898 and now sits beside the third, newer house on this site.

The Ivory Wilder House was built as a double house at 1 Hubbardston Road in 1842. As was the custom among thrifty New Englanders, this house was made with "used" lumber; in this case, taken from a late eighteenth-century inn known as the Richardson Tavern. From 1842 to 1885, Ivory Wilder lived in the half of the house that is still standing. Mr. Wilder, who served as Princeton's postmaster, operated the post office here. The other half of this double house, now missing, was used to accommodate the minister of the Congregational Church until 1870, when a parsonage was built. Ezra Hayward bought and moved the "missing half" to 7 Hubbardston Road in 1871, where it burned down in 1908. Marguerite Davis, a descendant of Ivory Wilder, operated Princeton's telephone exchange from the Wilder House after 1910. The exchange had been in the Wachusett Hotel, but that burned down in 1910. This late Georgian-style house faces the town common. It has had four additions to the original structure, including a nineteenth-century, one-and-a-half-story ell with a brick foundation and side-gabled roof.

The Rufus Davis House as it appeared in the late nineteenth century. By 1908, it had burned to the ground. *Princeton Historical Society.*

The Frederick Bryant House at 7 Hubbardston Road is a replacement for the 1842 "missing half" of Ivory Wilder's double house that was moved to this site in 1871. This house half was enlarged and used as a boardinghouse when it was owned by the Mountain Home Corporation of Boston. That all ended when it burned to the ground in 1908. Frederick Bryant bought the property and built his house in 1910. The entrance sits under a deep portico with Tuscan columns and a decorative balustrade on its roof. There is a similar porch across the left side of the house. The 1910 workshop and barn are both visible from the road and from the Boylston Burial Ground.

The Eleanor Howe Davis House is possibly the third building to stand at 5 Hubbardston Road. In 1882, town selectman Rufus Davis built a large three-story house with a mansard roof that burned to the ground in 1908. The house standing here today was built on the same foundation in 1908 by John C.F. Mirick, a local builder and descendant of one of Princeton's founding families. This may have been one of the first houses in Princeton with indoor plumbing. Rufus Davis's daughter Isabel lived in this house until the 1940s. It was built in the Colonial Revival style with a hipped roof and a deep portico supported by Tuscan columns.

A portrait of David
Hoyt Gregory,
founder of D.H.
Gregory & Co.
*Princeton Historical
Society.*

   The D.H. Gregory & Co. Store at 2 Mountain Road has a long and varied
history. The Princeton House File shows that Lieutenant Governor Moses
Gill built this property on the present common around 1775. Sometime
later, the town bought the building for a Baptist parsonage, and in 1802 the
Baptist minister, Reverend James Murdock, purchased the parsonage.
   David Hoyt Gregory was an employee in the store of Blake & Allen. In
1841, he bought the business and the property, which he renamed D.H.
Gregory & Co. The Gregory family ran this business until 1942. A post
office was located here from 1866 until the 1980s, when postal service
was relocated to Post Office Place. Later, after David Gregory no longer
owned the business, the store was sold to Malcolm and Ruth Chase and
was operated as the Village Store. The original house/store is a modified
Georgian vernacular style. The mansard roof was added around 1870.

The D.H. Gregory & Co. Store in the 1940s, when there was also a Mobil gas station on the premises. *Princeton Historical Society.*

After the original eighteenth-century house was converted to commercial use, several changes were made, including the addition of apartments and multiple entrances. This building also housed a restaurant until 2001 and is a complex of five attached ells.

The house currently at 6 Mountain Road was built in 1874 for Josiah D. Gregory, son of David H. Gregory, whose general store, D.H. Gregory & Co., was next door. Josiah Gregory worked in the family business from an early age and later served as Princeton's postmaster from 1889 to 1915 and town clerk from 1915 until his death in 1925. The Gregory family maintained ownership of the house until 1949. This is a three-story, Second Empire–style house with a mansard roof with pedimented dormers on all sides.

The Reverend Samuel Clarke House is now the oldest surviving residential building on the town common that has always been used as a family home. The house was built in 1819 at 10 Mountain Road for the Reverend Samuel Clarke (1791–1856), minister of the Congregational Church. It was built on the north side of the town common and was moved in 1838 to make way for the third Congregational meetinghouse (which was also later relocated). Phineas E. Gregory, father and business partner of

The Reverend Samuel Clarke House, oldest surviving residential building on the common.
Princeton Historical Society.

David H. Gregory, bought the Clarke house in 1845. His descendants kept the property in the family until 1958. This is a Federal-style house with a slate roof and an attached 1925 barn.

THE GREEK REVIVALS ON GREGORY HILL ROAD

There were five Greek Revival–style homes built next to one another on Gregory Hill Road during the peak years of this style, 1824 to 1844. Together, they are a treasure-trove of this graceful, early nineteenth-century style so characteristic of New England. Greek Revivals are easy to spot. You can see the references to classical antiquity in their pilasters, sidelights topped by a classical entablature and gable-front façades. All five of these buildings are now private homes. Four of them are connected to the Beaman family. Gamaliel Beaman arrived in the Massachusetts Bay Colony in 1635. The intrepid Mr. Beaman and his family braved the wilderness of this region and helped to settle the nearby town of Lancaster in 1659.

Red Bars Farm at 14 is one of the earliest of the five Greek Revival houses on Gregory Hill Road. It is also one of the largest properties in Princeton Center. The house was built, probably by Ward Nicholas Boylston, in 1824 for a tenant farmer. Edson Beaman was thought to be one of its earliest residents. The name Red Bars Farm was associated with this property while it was owned by Nathan Reed, who probably built the two barns and the shed. Nathan Reed and his descendants owned the property until the 1960s. Red Bars Farm is a front-gabled house with a Greek Revival entryway with pilasters and sidelights topped by a simple classical entablature. The house is set on a granite foundation. The free-standing east barn was built in 1870 by Nathan Reed. The west barn, with its gable end, facing the road, was built around 1900 to replace an earlier structure. This property, with its broad expanse of land, still has the appearance of a farm and is still a working farm, actively haying. It is set on a ten-acre landscape of meadows and woodlands.

David H. Gregory sold the land at 11 Gregory Hill Road to Edson Beaman in 1845. Beaman had already built a Greek Revival house there. It is a gable-front house with a Greek Revival entryway with pilasters and sidelights topped by a simple classical entablature. It has a side-gabled ell and is set on a granite foundation. According to tax records, Dr. Oscar Howe (1830–1911) purchased the property in 1866 as Princeton's first and only resident dentist at the time. The story of Dr. Howe's office is told later in this chapter.

The Nathan Danforth House at 13 Gregory Hill Road is the last of the adjacent Greek Revival–style homes built on Gregory Hill Road. It was built by Edson Beaman in 1844. In November 1845, he conveyed (for $600) the house to Nathan Danforth, a shoemaker. Danforth held the property for nearly thirteen years, until 1858, at which time it was sold to David H. Gregory and his brother, Phineas E. Gregory. This house is set farther back off the road than its neighbors. It, too, has a granite foundation and characteristic Greek Revival features. Later in the nineteenth century, two large bay windows were added, along with a wraparound full front porch and an ell. A large barn was also added sometime between 1871 and 1898.

Another member of the Beaman family is responsible for the Merriam/Beaman House at 15 Gregory Hill Road. In April 1842, Princeton merchant David H. Gregory conveyed about one acre of land on the north side of "the road to Sterling" to yeomen (working farmers) Alfred Beaman and Marshall Merriam. They began building the current house within a year or so, and records suggest that they may have built it as a "duplex." Beaman, however, did not retain his ownership very long. In 1844, he sold his undivided half interest in the overall property for $492 to Phineas E. Gregory. Gregory is shown living on the property on the 1857 and 1870 maps, and he may have occupied at least part of the house as early as 1844. In the late nineteenth century, ownership of the house was shared by Eliza and Sarah Davis and George and Eliza Folger. In 1883, the Folgers used their half of the building as the town's public library while the Goodnow Memorial Library was being built. The two sides of the house had separate ownership until 1919. This house is unusually wide for the Greek Revival period. Its deeply recessed center entrance with sidelights was added at a later time. It also has a wide barn that was built in 1842. That, too, is in the Greek Revival style with a period cornice and vertical plank siding.

The only house in this group not known to be attributed to the Beaman family is the Samuel Griffin House at 21 Gregory Hill Road. It was built in the Greek Revival style between 1830 and 1836. Little is known about its builder, Samuel Griffin. In the early twentieth century, the property was acquired by the Mason family, who still own it. This house has three additions of unknown dates and a simple porch. The large barn was built before 1870 and was probably an original part of the property.

The classic Merriam/Beaman Greek Revival house at 15 Gregory Hill Road. *Princeton Historical Society.*

TO YOUR HEALTH: MEDICAL STORIES

Princeton's history of medical care for its residents goes back to its earliest days. Some of the most interesting stories these buildings have to tell are about the places where medical care was offered and the medical cures promoted—here are their stories.

The Stratton-West House at 19 Hubbardston Road has a particularly convoluted history. It was built in 1792 and is believed to have been moved to its current site in 1834 by John Stratton and purchased by Dr. West in 1861. To further complicate the story, it was remodeled from 1855 to 1861 and again in 1874. The core of the building was the original Schoolhouse No.1, built on Mountain Road near the first meetinghouse, which replaced the town's first (1774) schoolhouse when it burned down. In 1834, John Stratton bought Schoolhouse No.1 and used a team of oxen to move it to this site. He placed it on the foundation of an earlier building and converted it to use as a home.

Dr. Joseph West, Princeton's local doctor, graduated from Harvard Medical School in 1848. He was a trusted medical advisor and wise counselor to the residents of the town and many transient visitors until his death in 1887. He added the ell, which he used as his medical office, and the barn, which held the horses and carriage he needed to make house calls. In 1874, Dr. West updated the house to include a then fashionable mansard roof.

In the early twentieth century, the West family created an art studio in the top level of the barn, along with a gift shop and tearoom. The original house

The house at 19 Hubbardston Road when it belonged to Dr. West. *Princeton Historical Society.*

The town's beloved Dr. West in his carriage, perhaps making a house call. *Princeton Historical Society.*

is a mansard-roofed modified Georgian, with dentils under the cornice. The West family owned this house until 1965.

As mentioned earlier, in 1866 Dr. Oscar Howe (1830–1911) bought the Greek Revival house that Edson Beaman built at 11 Gregory Hill Road. Dr. Howe added a small, one-story wooden office for his dental practice next to the house five years before he bought the house. The office was moved from the roadside farther back on the property in the 1980s. It remained Princeton's only dental office for fifty years. It is interesting to note that Dr. Howe was one of the first dentists in the area to use laughing gas.

Dr. Elisha Sears Lewis bought the lot at 18 Mountain Road in 1908 to build himself a home. He had been practicing medicine in Princeton for several years by then, specializing in European spa treatments such as hydrotherapy. He bought a local spring to provide pure water for his patients and formed a partnership with his neighbor, Prentice C. Doolittle, to bottle and sell Wachusett Mountain Spring Water.

In 1914, Dr. Lewis built his sanatorium facility at 20 Mountain Road. He based his plan on what he saw when he visited European health spas. He named his new facility the Princeton Nauheim Institution and promoted popular European treatments such as hydrotherapy and electrical and

An advertisement for the Wachusett Mountain Spring Water sold by Dr. Elisha Sears and P.C. Doolittle. *Princeton Historical Society.*

ultraviolet light treatments. These were, at the time, considered treatments for chronic ailments such as heart disease, high blood pressure, asthma, bronchitis, diabetes, rheumatism, anemia, gout, hysteria, hypochondria and more. Dr. Lewis was assisted by his wife, Catherine, with the care of his patients. Catherine organized local residents when the flu pandemic of 1918 struck. As a result of her efforts, none of Princeton's flu patients died. In 1929, Dr. Lewis sold the sanatorium and his house but continued to treat patients in Princeton until his death in 1955.

Prentice C. Doolittle was a well-known citizen who served as a selectman, undertaker, horse trader, contractor and builder. He is remembered for his partnership with Dr. Elisha Sears Lewis. From 1883 to 1909, Doolittle also contributed to Princeton's summer hotel trade by operating the Wachusett Coach Line to transport summer visitors arriving by train. He used the facilities of his coach business to store the town's fire engine in his barn. His home, built around 1880 at 19 Mountain Road, is a hipped-roof, wood-frame house just north of the Goodnow Memorial Library. It appears that it was originally Italianate in style, but many of those characteristic trim elements have been lost over time. Its wraparound porch has been replaced by a deck, and a one-story ell was built at some time.

In 1894, Dr. Charles E. Parker had the house at 15 Worcester Road built for himself as a summer residence. In 1900, Dr. Parker moved to Princeton permanently and established a medical practice. This large Queen Anne–style home was designed by architect C.T. Hartshorn, well known for his summer cottages. The house has a typical Queen Anne complex roofscape and wraparound porch, as well as a matching carriage house with a cupola and weather vane.

STAY A WHILE: PRINCETON'S HOTELS AND SUMMER HOMES

Princeton's heyday as a summer resort has ended but the town still enjoys many trophies of this era. The popularity of the large hotels encouraged wealthy people to build large summer homes with spectacular scenic views. That, in turn, encouraged the less affluent to build more modest summer homes or to "modernize" the homes they already had in more fashionable styles. The following are some reminders of those glorious days in the Princeton Center area.

Charles G. Washburn was one of Princeton's most notable residents. He was a U.S. congressman and founder of the Washburn Wire Company in Worcester. He built the grand property known as Hilltop as a summer home in 1899–1900 as a suitable place to entertain his friend President Theodore Roosevelt.

This property, at 30 Mountain Road, remained in the family until it was sold to Roy Wall in 1950. Mr. Wall established and operated the Meeting House Restaurant in the house. In the 1970s, subsequent owners continued to use it as a restaurant but changed its name to the Inn at Princeton. The house is a very large, rambling, Shingle-style building on a hilly spot overlooking the Boston skyline. Its broad, Tuscan-style veranda is evidence of its original use as a grand summer retreat. It is once again a private residence, but as of this writing Teddy Roosevelt has not scheduled another visit.

Samuel Lackey built at least part of his double house at 21 Mountain Road in 1819. It appears that the two halves were joined together sometime before 1870. Charles Washburn bought this property around the turn of the twentieth century, when he was enjoying his large summer home across the road. Mrs. Washburn's chauffeur, Liberty, lived there until 1940 or so. This small house shows evidence of having been a double structure (the south side of the house is taller than the north side) and has two inside staircases. There is now a shed dormer and a two-story addition on the rear. The barn was built sometime after 1898.

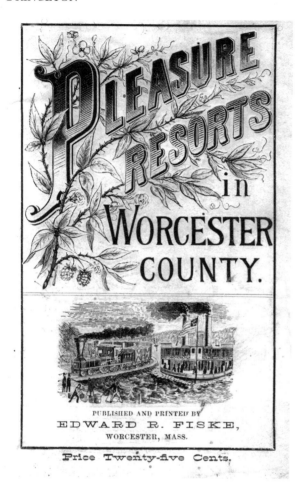

A booklet promoting the pleasure resorts in Princeton and featuring Princeton's hotels. *Princeton Historical Society*.

Number 24 Mountain Road is an eclectic collection of four buildings now known as the Manor Apartments. Like other properties on Mountain Road, it was originally built as a "summer cottage" in 1903 for wealthy owners Hamilton and Elizabeth Perkins of Boston. The Perkinses sold the property in 1925. In 1938, a new owner converted the property into an inn and called it the Princeton Manor. By 1948, another owner, Emry Swan, changed its use again and turned it into the Princeton Manor Convalescent and Rest Home. The next change was more violent when, in 1967, the property suffered a fire that resulted in the loss of lives. After that, it was sold again and converted into apartments in the 1970s. There is a sign identifying the Manor Apartments in front of the barn. Today, the property offers eight residential units for rent.

The property encompasses a house, barn, cabin, shed and dry-laid stone walls. The house is the largest building and appears to be a series of four smaller attached buildings. The original 1903 structure is a Shingle-style house with a very wide, curved bay window. The large barn was built at the same time as the original house. It is distinctive in that it stands on a raised rubble stone foundation and displays an eyebrow dormer over the barn doors. The small Bungalow-style cabin was built in the 1930s or '40s, when the original house was in commercial use. It, too, sits on a raised rubble stone foundation and features a deep open porch and a bay window.

The Harry Delano House is within the area that was the original town center. At 58 Mountain Road, it is on the site of the first and second Congregational meetinghouses, which stood from 1763 to 1840 and were owned by the Town of Princeton until the late 1800s. Even though the meetinghouse (now known as the Congregational Church) was built on the town common in 1838, the decision to sell this land was a long-fought battle.

When the property was finally sold, it was encumbered by a restriction stating that any house built on the property must be worth at least $5,000. As that was a princely sum at the time, Princeton was fortunate to attract Harry C. Delano as that "prince." He was a Bostonian, wealthy enough to build this house as a summer home in 1902. Like their neighbors, the Washburns and Perkinses, the Delano family did not use the house for very long. They rented it out for several summers and sold it in 1917.

In 1905, Mrs. Edward Padgham opened Woodland Cottage at 11 Prospect Street as a summer guesthouse. It offered guests the amenity of a clear view of the Boston skyline from the second-floor porch. Built in the late Queen Anne style, this house features a spindle-balustrade wraparound porch and Queen Anne–style windows. The property accommodated ten to twelve guests and housed a barbershop in the basement. When the new Princeton Center School opened in 1906, Woodland Cottage was home to several young, unmarried teachers. In the 1930s, the house was struck by lightning but did not burn down.

Seth and Mary Nichols were interested in innovative, scientific farming practices. They built the Seth Nichols House at 20 Worcester Road in 1906–07 as a summer home for themselves and a farm for their Guernsey cows, chickens, orchards and gardens. Their large, English country–style house sits on a seventeen-acre lot that was the site of an earlier property known as the Windmill House. During World War I, they used the third floor as a workroom for making bandages and other goods for the relief of the war casualties in Europe. After Mr. Nichols died, Dr. Charles Wheeler bought the property as a summer home and farm use was discontinued.

The cottage at 26 Worcester Road was built in 1928 by Dr. Charles Wheeler on land that was part of the Windmill House farm next door. Dr. Wheeler

Mrs. Edward Padgham's Woodland Cottage guesthouse, which featured a view of Boston from the veranda. *Princeton Historical Society*.

Looking toward Princeton center with the Wachusett House hotel in the distance. This photo was taken before 1910, when the hotel burned down. *Princeton Historical Society*.

owned the Windmill House farm and he built this Bungalow-style house as a farmer's cottage. It has since become a separate, single-home property.

The house at 23 Worcester Road was built in 1875 by Isaac Franklin Thompson when he retired from his career as a hotelier. Mr. Thompson was co-manager of the Wachusett House hotel from 1857 to 1860 and owner of the Prospect House hotel from 1860 to 1874. His house, it seems, was not finished with the hospitality business in mind, although subsequent owners operated a restaurant and tearoom here from 1937 to 1951. This house is notable for its Greek Revival/Italianate style and large barn.

AND A FEW MORE

Princeton has an embarrassment of riches in terms of historic properties. The richness of this heritage means that some are difficult to categorize, such as the following.

The 1869 parsonage at 22 Mountain Road was home to fourteen Congregationalist ministers. It continued to serve as a parsonage until the 1980s. This front-gabled, Greek Revival property boasts a large barn that features the same trim style as the house.

Thomas Allen built the bungalow at 32 Allen Hill Road in 1918 across the road from his own baronial home, constructed in 1894. The 1898 map of Princeton shows that Mr. Allen owned a great deal of land on both sides of Allen Hill Road, which was named for him. This bungalow is most unusual in that it is the only "mail order" house in the district, designed and prefabricated by the Aladdin Company. According to Eleanor Allen, the house was built for her brother, Thomas Allen Jr., and his wife, and Eleanor's mother also used it as a respite from the busy life at the "Big House."

Prentice C. Doolittle apparently constructed the property at 16 Boylston Avenue as a rental unit in 1901. Perhaps this was made possible by the success of his Wachusett Mountain Spring Water business. This small, side-gabled, Bungalow-style house has a deep front porch. The property includes a barn, built a few years earlier than the house.

Thomas Allen sold the site at 33 Mountain Road to R.S. Hamilton, a Princeton builder. Shortly after building this small L-shaped house, Mr. Hamilton sold it to Theo Brown of Illinois to use as a three-season home for his family. The Browns continued to live here for at least thirty years, and it stayed in the Brown family until the 1980s. This house is one of the last structures built in Princeton Center. There have been very few changes made to the exterior since it was built in 1937.

John C.F. Mirick lived at 5 Prospect Street, which he built around 1899. This local builder, who designed and built homes in Princeton around the turn of the twentieth century, also designed a chapel in East Princeton and remodeled the third Summit House hotel on Wachusett Mountain. The civic-minded Mr. Mirick served as a selectman and town moderator. His daughter, Ethel Mirick, lived in this house until her death in 1964. Miss Mirick, a teacher, was the first woman to serve on the Princeton School Committee. This hipped-roof, late Victorian/Colonial Revival house stands on a rubble stone foundation and features a Palladian window and an attached barn.

The Brooks-Goddard Slaughterhouse and Carriage House at 27 Worcester Road was built on the site of the former Brooks-Goddard property. This house, built in 1874–75, is of the Second Empire style, the most popular style in Princeton during the 1870s both for new construction and for "modernizing" older buildings. It started out as a mansard-roof, wood-frame farm outbuilding used as a slaughterhouse. The main floor of the building has a relatively high ceiling and you can still see the foundation from the back. The first time it was used as a residence was in the early 1940s.

Alexander Bullock was an executive with the Massachusetts Mutual Life Insurance Company in Worcester. He and his brothers spent their childhood summers in Princeton in an 1870s house that their father built. In 1906, Alexander built a house across the road at 1 Worcester Road. The Roman Catholic Diocese of Worcester bought this property in 1955 and built the Prince of Peace Church at the adjacent corner of Worcester and Gregory Hill Roads. Before then, the congregation met at the Goodnow Memorial Building. This house has been used as the church rectory since the church was built in 1964.

GHOSTS: SOME INTERESTING STRUCTURES NOT ALL THERE ANY MORE

Many structures are considered "lost" when they are torn down, burned down or just plain forgotten. However, they may still have something to tell us about ourselves and how we got here. Although most of Princeton's "ghosts" are visible only in the mind's eye, there are a few in Princeton Center that we can still see in the light of day.

In 1912, Princeton voted to create a municipal streetlighting plant behind Bagg Hall. By 1914, the Princeton Light Department Building was operating and powering 130 electric streetlights, as well as providing power for fifty-six customers. This tiny, one-story brick building was not replaced until sometime in the 1950s. It still stands on top of the steep slope of the hill rising from Hubbardston Road to Bagg Hall. The door is gone now, and the building is vacant, overgrown and largely forgotten.

Not all ghosts are human. The Brooks-Goddard Dog House at 23 Worcester Road may once have served as a cupola. It was built in 1874–75 by John Brooks Jr. for his Hillside Farm. This was no ordinary doghouse. It was designed to match the Second Empire–style Brooks-Goddard House next door. Although the house was demolished in 1936, the doghouse lives on. It was moved to the Audubon Society and then to the Antique Auto Museum, formerly on Worcester Road. After 1959, the doghouse was restored and returned it to its original location.

On the northeast side of the former D.H. Gregory store, there are remnants of a small, one-story, wood and stone structure. It was built in the late nineteenth century as an acetylene gas generating plant to supply gas

The sites of the Wachusett House and the long-gone Thomas Gill house and barn, as seen from the common. *Princeton Historical Society*.

Wachusett House, shuttered and closed, after a spectacular ice storm. *Princeton Historical Society.*

lighting for the store and several nearby buildings. The precise age of this gas plant is uncertain and it is in poor condition. Even so, as a survivor of its type, it is unique in Princeton.

Dingman Park is a small public area at the intersection of Boylston Avenue and Worcester Road. Although the park is too new to be called historic, it is the site of two historic lodging houses. John Brooks Sr. built the Wachusett House Tavern (originally known as Wachusett House) there in 1822. He moved it next door around 1847 and it is still standing today at 7 Boylston Avenue. John Brooks built a second Wachusett House in 1847. In 1859, he sold that building to Phineas Beaman, who expanded the building and ran it as a popular summer hotel from 1866 to 1880. It remained a hotel until 1910, when it burned to the ground. Remnants of the foundation of the second Wachusett House hotel, its barn and granite stone wall, all circa 1847, still stand in Dingman Park. Dingman Park also features a six-foot-wide, beehive-shaped brick cistern that appears to date to the late nineteenth century.

CHAPTER THREE

RIGHT AROUND THE CORNER

The Russell Corner Story

Yes, everything is just right around Russell Corner! It's a perfect gem of historic architecture in a pristine pastoral setting. Yet the reasons for Russell Corner's early development were not entirely pastoral. Transportation is at the core of Russell Corner's founding because Princeton's earliest road goes right through it.

In 1670, long before Princeton was founded, the Bay Path was laid out by the colonial government to open new land to settlement and to connect Boston to the Connecticut River Valley settlements. The Bay Path crossed through Princeton, coming from Sterling and following what is now Houghton Road. Princeton's first inn was established on this road by Joshua Wilder. Merriam Road and Gregory Hill Road were among Princeton's earliest transportation routes, connecting Russell Corner with the center of Princeton.

Russell Corner was listed in the National Register of Historic Places on February 22, 2006, by the National Park Service. The district covers a total land area of approximately sixty-seven acres and includes only twelve houses. These generous lot sizes reflect Princeton's historic character as an agricultural community. The Russell Corner Historic District is a small group of architecturally noteworthy buildings, built over about eighty years. Nine of the buildings in Russell Corner were built from 1748 to 1830.

The buildings in Russell Corner were constructed of either wood or brick and represent well-preserved examples of Georgian and Federal architectural styles. These styles are seen in the characteristic center chimneys, symmetrical fenestration patterns and, most especially, in the classic doorways. Although Princeton was a rural town, its architecture of this period is remarkably sophisticated. Historian George Baumgardner observed, "Asher Benjamin's

Today trees block the view, but in 1902 there was an unobstructed view from the Princeton Golf Club at Russell Corner to Princeton Center. *Princeton Historical Society.*

simplification of the ornamental detail of the Adam brothers is evident on many houses today. If one may judge from the extant architecture, 1790–1825 were the halcyon years." Asher Benjamin was a famous architect and author of the influential *American Builder's Companion, 1827.*

Eight of the twelve houses are located close to one another along Merriam and Gregory Hill Roads. The proximity of these houses formed an important commercial and civic center during the years 1748 to 1883. It was a center for businesses, which included two stores, two taverns, a post office and a meeting hall. A schoolhouse served the families in the area.

Russell Corner got its name from Charles Russell, who built his store in 1822. Russell had a long career in public service, holding numerous local and statewide offices. By the turn of the twentieth century, Russell's children and grandchildren occupied five of the residences in Russell Corner. The association with the Russell family continued well into the twentieth century and two of his descendants live there today.

THE EARLY DAYS

The General Court was proven wise to have granted land to Joshua Wilder in the hopes of encouraging new settlements. During the last half of the eighteenth century, Princeton's growth increased 400 percent in less than thirty years. The population grew from 284 residents in 1765 to 1,016 inhabitants in 1791. In 1793, historian Peter Whitney observed of Princeton:

> *In a little more than 30 years from its incorporation, Princeton is become very considerable among the towns of the [Worcester] county. It has surprisingly increased in number and in wealth. The land is…exceedingly well adapted to pasturage and the growth of English grass. Hence the finest of beef is fatted here, and vast quantities of butter and cheese are produced…we must judge the people are very industrious. Many of their houses are large and elegant.*

By the late 1750s, Princeton had about twenty-five homesteads that were widely spread within the nineteen thousand acres of its boundaries. Princeton's first "town center" was located in Russell Corner years before the first meetinghouse was built on Meeting House Hill. Here Lieutenant Abijah Moore hosted a small group of men and women in his home and tavern. These people came together to carry out the necessary business of the small community and to worship.

Abijah Moore came from the town of Sudbury, one of the earliest towns to be settled on the western edge of the Massachusetts Bay Colony. By 1748, he followed many of his Sudbury neighbors and moved farther west to the wilderness that was Princeton. He built his house at 16 Merriam Road, and by 1750 he was an innkeeper. With the construction of the first official road in Princeton in 1762, it is likely that Moore was successful as an innkeeper as more people traveled west. The small community began holding religious services in Lieutenant Moore's house in October 1759, and on Christmas Eve of the same year, the first district meeting was held there. The small congregation continued to hold meetings in his home until the first meetinghouse was built on Meeting House Hill in 1762. When the first meetinghouse opened in 1763, with its dual function as a house of worship and as the town house for local government, the official center of town shifted about a half mile northwest of Moore's Tavern to the intersection of Merriam and Mountain Roads at the top of Meeting House Hill.

Lieutenant Moore sold his property to Joseph Sargent in 1765, and the tavern continued to operate until around 1780, when the property passed into the Temple and Reed families. At this time it was used as a farmhouse with a large barn. Thomas Hastings Russell bought it from Joseph A. Reed and continued to use the property as a farm. In the 1890s, Russell leased the old Moore homestead farm to a tenant for about twenty years but later

Abijah Moore and a small group of early settlers held the first district meeting in this house on December 24, 1759. *Princeton Historical Society.*

converted the house into a summer residence for one of his daughters. The house has remained in the family until the present time.

When Thomas Russell took ownership, he moved the side ell to the rear and built a wraparound porch on the front with a gazebo on the left side of the porch. During Thomas Russell's ownership, this house was known as the Yellow House. Details of early construction include massive chimney foundations in the cellar, pegged rafters in the attic, a huge living room fireplace with a Dutch oven, wide floorboards, old beams and wall paneling.

In about 1760, Abijah Moore was joined in town by another settler from Sudbury when Peter Goodnow built a new house a short distance from Moore's Tavern. Peter Goodnow, born in Sudbury, was married in 1736 to Dorothy Moore, sister of Abijah Moore. When they moved to Princeton, it is not surprising that they chose to live near family, since there were so few people living in Princeton at the time. Peter Goodnow quickly became active in town affairs and was elected selectman in 1760, the same year he moved to Princeton. Sadly, his wife Dorothy died that year. One year later, in 1761, Peter married Ann Mosman of Lancaster and was elected assessor, district treasurer and warden. On November 20, 1763, three years after leaving Sudbury, he "was dismissed from the Sudbury church to the service of erecting with others a church following in Princeton." Peter Goodnow was faithful to this charge. He was among a small group of Princeton men

Moore's Tavern at Russell Corner was adapted as a summer home in the early twentieth century. The ell was moved and a wraparound porch was added. *Joyce Anderson*.

to sign the 1764 covenant, which established the legitimacy of the new congregation that was to worship in the new meetinghouse. Peter Goodnow remained in Princeton until 1779, when he moved to Hubbardston, where he spent the remaining years of his life.

A portion of the original Goodnow House is incorporated into 49 Gregory Hill Road. The other portion of the house was moved closer to Merriam Road. Today nothing remains of the house that was moved, although there is a set of stone steps that leads to an area where the house may have been. The steps are located on the southwest side of the Princeton Land Trust property, near Merriam Road. Francis Blake wrote about the Goodnow House in his *History of Princeton*: "Peter Goodnow's house was divided and moved to a site on the southwest side of Merriam Road." The stairs are a visible reminder of what may have been in this vicinity at Russell Corner.

Tax records show that sometime around 1760, a third house was built at the corner of Merriam and Mirick Roads. Its original owner is unknown, but a part of that structure is incorporated into the John Russell House at 28 Merriam Road. The district's long association with the Russell family began when John Russell came to Princeton from Littleton, Massachusetts,

One of the earliest houses in Russell Corner, the John Russell House was enlarged several times and served as a tavern. *Princeton Historical Society.*

with his wife, Eunice, and infant daughter, Anna. The house served as an inn and was run by John Russell. John soon enlarged the house to accommodate his growing family of four more children and to provide overnight accommodations for travelers. After John Russell's early death, his widow and young family remained in the house while Captain Samuel Stevenson took over the retail business. Stevenson married Anna Russell in 1808. Four years later, he was appointed Princeton's first postmaster.

The Georgian-style house currently belongs to a descendant of John Russell and has remained in the same family since 1787, when John Russell built a portion of it. It is one of the two earliest houses built in Russell Corner. This house was originally a one-story, one- or two-bay house with an end chimney and was enlarged to its present two-and-a-half-story height and five-bay width in 1787.

In 1765, the newly established village at Russell Corner gained a fourth family when Adonijah Howe built a log cabin northeast of Merriam Road on what is now Bullock Lane. Howe lived in the log cabin for thirty-five years and he and his wife raised ten children there. He began building a new Georgian-style house at 28 Bullock Lane, but he died before he could finish

In 1764, Adonijah Howe built a log cabin for his wife and ten children at 26 Bullock Lane. This house replaced the cabin in 1800. *Princeton Historical Society.*

it. After his death in 1800, his son Adonijah Jr. finished the house. It still graces the far eastern end of Bullock Lane.

Adonijah Howe Sr. is buried in Meeting House Cemetery, and the inscription on his gravestone reads, "Chorister of the singing and Deacon of the church 33 years in this town." His son Adonijah Howe Jr. was also active in the church as a deacon and shared his father's devotion to the church choir. In 1812, after living in the house for eleven years, he sold it and built another one in 1812, at the intersection of Merriam Road and Bullock Lane.

AND THEN THE RUSSELLS SETTLED IN

Russell Corner owes more than just its name to the first Russell to settle here. Russell Corner waned as a center of town activity in the first few decades of the nineteenth century as the new town center began to emerge in the area that is now Princeton Center. New regional transportation systems, such as the

The ell of Peter Goodnow's homestead at 49 Gregory Hill Road was incorporated into the house that Charles Russell built for his bride in 1815. *Princeton Historical Society.*

Royalston–Worcester Stagecoach Line in 1822 and the Boston–Barre Turnpike in 1826, ensured that the newly formed Princeton Center would remain the official civic and commercial center of town. Russell Corner would acquire a new identity with Charles Russell, the youngest member of the Russell family.

When John Russell died at the age of thirty-seven, Charles, his youngest son, was only six years old. Charles found a mentor in Samuel Stevenson, his sister Anna's husband who had taken over John's store after his death. Naturally, Samuel had a great influence on young Charles and taught him to be a shopkeeper. Charles married Persis Hastings, granddaughter of Edward Goodnow, in 1815, and in the same year he purchased Peter Goodnow's old homestead on Goodnow Lane. Charles built a Federal-style house for his bride and incorporated Peter Goodnow's 1760 house and 1771 ell into the new structure. He copied the six-panel front door with pilasters and transom light from the 1786 Edward Goodnow House that now serves as the visitor center at Wachusett Meadows, Massachusetts Audubon Society.

The barn with double doors was built in 1824 and is attached to the northeast end of the ell. For many years, when the barn doors were open, it was possible to see the sign for Charles Russell's store hanging inside. The sign was donated to the Princeton Historical Society some years ago and now hangs proudly in its collection.

In 1817, at the age of twenty-four, Charles Russell became Princeton's postmaster and succeeded his brother-in-law, Samuel Stevenson, as owner of the village store. In 1822–23, Russell and his business partner, Ephraim Mirick, built a new brick store and post office at the southwest corner of Merriam and Gregory Hill Roads.

Charles Russell was first and foremost a farmer, as were many of his neighbors. During the late eighteenth and early nineteenth centuries, much of the land in this region was cleared of old growth forests for lumber and charcoal. The open land created fields for grazing, and by 1831, Princeton had nearly three thousand head of cattle. In addition to producing food, these animals also generated several early manufacturing enterprises in town, including tanneries and shoe manufacturers. Princeton, being the self-reliant town that it was, took full advantage of the tanneries and a short distance away, in West Village, supplied two shoe manufacturing businesses. Agriculture remained the mainstay of Princeton's economy well into the nineteenth century and even into the twentieth century. Fred Mason, who grew up in Russell Corner, at 6 Merriam Road, recalled in 1988:

> *I remember at the end of World War I my father raised all the food that we ate. We even raised wheat, which is unusual for this part of the country. He plowed the fields himself, and we also planted orchards, big asparagus plants, strawberries, raspberries. We made a living that way.*

Charles Russell was also a successful businessman. Before turning fifty, he held a succession of local and statewide elected offices, served as a deacon in his church and earned appointments to several important boards and commissions. Russell found time for public service, holding a series of elected and appointed offices at both the local and state levels from the 1820s through the 1840s. By the mid-nineteenth century, Charles Russell was well known in Boston. By the age of thirty-three, he had been elected a representative to the state legislature and later a representative of Worcester County in the state senate. He later served three years on the Governor's Council. After his political career ended, he became the surveyor of the Boston Customs House, supervising the unloading of ships entering Boston Harbor. For most of his working life, he lived in Boston or Cambridge for much of the year, only spending summers in Princeton. His family looked after the Russell Corner store in his absence. He retired in 1860, and once again became a year-round resident of Princeton. Charles and Persis Russell were married

Thomas Hastings Russell and his wife, Maria Lousia Wiswell Russell, are seen sitting on the porch of their home sometime before 1892. *Deb and Charlie Cary.*

for sixty-seven years and had three children, Charles Theodore (known as Theodore), Thomas Hastings and Sarah Ann. In the 1880s, in the final years of their lives, Charles and his wife moved to Boston to live with their son Thomas. Charles Russell's son Theodore left his mark on Princeton as a young man in his senior year of college when he wrote home to his father suggesting that he (Theodore) write a history of Princeton:

> *I have a design by which I think I can make 50 or 60 dollars, which, for a particular purpose, would come in very opportune at this moment. I propose to write a concise history of Princeton: its settlement, geography, civil, political, and ecclesiastical matters, designed for the inhabitants and which will comprise about 100 pages and sell for 50 cents a copy…Would you interest yourself enough in the matter to [find out if] a subscription could be got up for 200 or 300 copies? I am inclined to be of the opinion that such a pamphlet would be popular in the town.*

That history was published the following year, in 1838. Copies of it can still be found in the collections of the Princeton Public Library, the Princeton Historical Society and the American Antiquarian Society Library in Worcester.

Both Thomas Russell and his brother, Theodore, graduated from Harvard College and Law School. In 1845, the brothers formed the Boston law firm of C.T. and T.H. Russell, which continued in business into the twentieth century. Three sons and one grandson subsequently joined the family firm. Theodore's son, William Eustis Russell, not only followed his father into the practice of law but also followed his grandfather into politics and was elected mayor of Cambridge and governor of Massachusetts for three terms. The brothers often summered in Russell Corner with their own families while maintaining an active law practice and residences in Boston and Cambridge.

Charles Russell established once-a-week rural free mail delivery in Princeton. As early as the 1820s, with an increasing number of people moving to Princeton, there was some discussion about relocating the post office to the new town center. Despite the increase in population, the main post office remained in Russell's store for some thirty years longer. In the late 1840s, several new branch post offices opened, including East Princeton in 1849. The main post office was not moved to Princeton Center until 1854, when it was established at Ivory Wilder's house in the center of town.

In 1822–23, not very far from his home at 49 Gregory Hill Road, Charles Russell built a square red brick building to house his store and post office, as well as a hall for public gatherings. It was two stories tall, with the store and post office on the first floor and a public meeting hall on the second floor. The store sold provisions and spices, fabrics and clothing, household goods, tobacco and rum, newspapers, school textbooks and copies of the *Old Farmer's Almanac*, among other goods. Above the store, the public meeting hall was used by organizations such as the Masonic Lodge and the Anti-Slavery Society. Charles Russell was a participant in both of these organizations. The second floor was also used for town social events. According to Katherine Poor, one of Russell's descendants, its "slung" floor was specially made for dancing.

By the summer of 1825, another house was built at 55 Gregory Hill Road in Russell Corner. Store owners Charles Russell and his partner, Ephraim Mirick, kept a diary titled "Notebook of Common Occurences." In this diary they recorded the comings and goings at Russell Corner. Little information is given as to the exact date this house was built, except for a reference in the notebook that read, "May 19, 1825, measured out the lot for Mrs. Hartwell's house." The diary began on April 1, 1825, and ended on Thursday, March 13, 1828. Mrs. Hartwell was the widow of Jonas Hartwell, who died in 1820. The Hartwells had six children and presumably they all lived in this Cape-style house. Charles Russell bought the property and bequeathed it to his son, Thomas H. Russell, who leased it out as a farmer's cottage about the time the old tavern of Abijah Moore (16 Merriam Road) was converted into a summer residence.

Between 1812 and 1825, three new residences were built in Russell Corner. In 1812, Adonijah Howe Jr. built a small house and blacksmith shop at the corner of Merriam Road and Bullock Lane. This house was replaced in the late 1820s by the one currently standing at 6 Merriam Road. It remained in the ownership of the Howe family until Harry Abijah Mason bought it in 1910. It has been in the Mason family ever since.

Joel Howe, interestingly not related to the Adonijah Howe family, purchased land from Joseph A. Reed in 1822. In 1823, he built a Federal-style brick house at 8 Merriam Road. Joel Howe was a blacksmith and built a barn next to his house, from which he operated his business. Formerly a resident of Holden, he moved to Princeton to marry Lydia Merriam, daughter of Amos Merriam. The Merriams had lived in Princeton since 1788 and it was Amos Merriam for whom the road was named. Amos was also a surveyor and was the mapmaker commissioned to plot the 1830 map of Princeton. Joel Howe maintained the blacksmith shop and contributed to the commercial life of the village. He sold his house and shop in 1836 to another blacksmith, Elisha Goddard.

As Princeton's population increased, so did the need for a new schoolhouse. In 1810, the Centre District school on Meeting House Hill was subdivided, with Russell Corner and West Village each getting a new schoolhouse. Until the new schoolhouses were built, the one on Meeting House Hill served all families living within a mile. This included the children of Russell Corner. That brought the total number of schoolhouses in town to nine. The Russell Corner schoolhouse was the first new building erected in Russell Corner in the nineteenth century. It was built in 1810 just southwest of the Goodnow-Russell House on what was then Goodnow Lane. The present structure at 43 Gregory Hill Road is the third school building to stand on this site. Like most of Princeton's schools, the original wood-frame building was reconstructed, in 1836, in brick. The brick schoolhouse was replaced again, in 1875, with a wood-frame building. In 1883, John Brooks converted the schoolhouse into a private residence.

By 1830, Amos Merriam's map of Princeton showed twelve schoolhouses with ten of them numbered. The school-age population continued to grow during this period. Charles Theodore Russell noted in his 1838 history of Princeton that 378 students attended school in Princeton, in a roughly fifty-fifty ratio of boys to girls. The children studied reading, writing, geography, arithmetic and grammar. Natural philosophy, chemistry, algebra and other advanced subjects were available for older students. Boys attended school in winter and girls in summer. Schoolhouse No. 1 served the children of Russell Corner until 1883, when Princeton's system of one-room schoolhouses was consolidated into the new Goodnow Memorial Building in Princeton Center.

SUMMER DAYS

As the summer resort era reached its zenith in Princeton in the late nineteenth and early twentieth centuries, six of the twelve buildings in Russell Corner had been converted into summer homes. Two of the oldest houses, at 16 and 19 Merriam Road, were altered in the late nineteenth century with the addition of porches that were popular at that time.

In 1860, Charles Russell retired from business and political life and closed his store at 19 Merriam Road. In about 1874, his son Thomas Russell converted the former store for use as a summer residence. After making renovations, he named it the Mansion House. In 1875, he added a then fashionable mansard roof, an octagonal cupola and paired cornice brackets below the mansard roof. His final flourish was the addition of a wraparound porch on three sides. These renovations changed the building from its former utilitarian state to one of grandeur and style.

In 1874, Charles Russell's store took on a new look when it was transformed into a summer mansion with a mansard roof, cupola and wraparound porch. *Deb and Charlie Cary*.

In 1875, Nathan Reed sold Russell the neighboring Locust Lawn Farm, which included Abijah Moore's old homestead at 16 Merriam Road, as well as other land southeast of Russell Corner. Reed apparently acquired or inherited Locust Lawn Farm and the old Moore homestead from his brother, Joseph P. Reed, who died in 1870. Their father, Major Joseph A. Reed, had purchased the old Moore homestead sometime in the early nineteenth century, as his name appears on the 1830 map.

Thomas Russell became Russell Corner's major landowner after his father's death in 1882. He inherited his grandfather John's house (28 Merriam Road), his father Charles's house (49 Gregory Hill Road) and a farmer's cottage at 55 Gregory Hill Road. With the inheritance of these houses, Russell established a family compound that remained a Princeton landmark for generations to come. Various family members used all five properties, either as permanent residences or as summer vacation homes, well into the twentieth century. For many years these buildings were known by their paint colors: the White House (49 Gregory Hill Road), the Yellow House (16 Merriam Road), the Gray House (19 Merriam Road) and the Brown House (28 Merriam Road).

As summer residences were gaining in popularity elsewhere in Princeton after the Civil War, the members of the Russell family continued to enjoy living at Russell Corner. Sometime in the late 1890s, the Russell family donated land on the east side of today's Sterling Road. The Russells used that land to enrich the social opportunities of life in Princeton with a golf course and clubhouse built in 1902.

At the end of the summer holiday, there was an annual Labor Day tournament held at the club. The rocky six-hole golf course, laced with stone walls, presented a challenge. After about twenty years of operation, the golf club closed as more people were able to travel to better courses in other towns. The golf club and the greens are no longer in existence and have become part of the landscape.

Katharine Poor, one of Thomas Russell's descendants, reminisced in 1988:

I've summered here all my life. The hotels were gone by the time I started coming to Princeton, and it was not as much of a fashionable place to stay. There were not as many activities going on in the center of town as there were in the early 1900s, but it was still exciting because there were 13 first cousins staying in Russell Corner when I was young. There were so many of us it was like a children's day camp. The weenie roast was a marvelous event that happened at the end of every summer. My aunt would gather the whole family, sometimes 75 strong, ranging in age from 2 months to 90

The Princeton Golf Club became a visitor attraction in the late 1890s. By the 1920s, it had closed as the automobile became popular. *Princeton Historical Society*.

In the early 1900s, four generations of the Charles Russell family reunited each summer at Russell Corner. *Deb and Charlie Cary*.

*years, and serve hot dogs, hamburgers, and corn on the cob under the oak
tree next to the tennis courts. I remember sitting on the edge of the croquet
lawn and singing. That was the finale of the whole summer. It was four
generations singing and playing together.*

When Adonijah Howe Sr. built his house at 26 Bullock Lane in 1800, the
lane had no name, and by 1898 it still remained unnamed. During the mid-
twentieth century, the lane had three successive names. First it was called
Magee Lane after Houston Magee, who owned the Howe farmhouse from
1905 to 1919. Then, in 1954, it was called Anthony Avenue after Edgar W.
Anthony, who owned the house well into the twentieth century. And finally,
in the 1960s, the lane was renamed Bullock Lane in honor of the family
whose association with Russell Corner had begun some forty years earlier,
with the arrival of Chandler Bullock.

Edgar Anthony sold the Howe House with approximately thirty-eight
acres of land to Chandler Bullock, an executive with the Massachusetts
Mutual Life Insurance Company in Worcester. Bullock grew up in Worcester
and first came to Princeton as a child. It was natural that he would make
his home in Princeton since his father, Colonel Augustus George Bullock,
built one of Princeton's earliest luxury summer homes in Princeton Center
in the 1870s. As adults, two of Colonel Bullock's sons continued the family
tradition of maintaining summer homes in Princeton. One son lived in
Princeton Center and the other on Bullock Lane.

It was Chandler Bullock's intention to use the Howe House as his summer
residence, but he decided to lease it instead. He eventually sold the house to
his cousin, Richard Bullock. Before selling the house, he built tennis courts
and initiated an annual Labor Day tennis tournament for Princeton residents
and visitors that continued until at least the late 1940s. After Chandler
Bullock sold the Howe House, he built the house at 8 Bullock Lane, in 1933,
as his summer residence.

By the 1930s, Princeton's heyday as a summer resort was waning.
Princeton residents Chandler Bullock and Oliver Chute built new houses
at a time when the country was just coming out of the Great Depression.
Their choice to build smaller homes may have been dictated by economic
stress. They were among the few to actually build anything in Princeton in
the 1930s. According to Judith Chute, Bullock's granddaughter, he found the
design for his house in an illustration in a Boston newspaper and ordered the
blueprints by mail. This early twentieth-century summer home is an example
of a vernacular "catalog house." It is distinctive as one of only two early
twentieth-century catalog homes in Russell Corner that were constructed

In 1935, Harris (DeeDee) Richardson, a descendant of John Russell, and Anne Beaman were partners at the annual Princeton Labor Day tennis tournament. Mr. Richardson was a World War II casualty while leading maneuvers at Hillsboro Army Air Field in Florida. *Princeton Historical Society.*

specifically as summer residences toward the end of Princeton's summer resort era. The house was built fully winterized but was never occupied year-round until after the Bullocks sold it in 1965. During the off-season, Bullock and his family lived in Worcester.

When Chandler Bullock built this summer residence, he subdivided a three-and-a-half-acre parcel between the old Howe farmhouse and his own brand-new home for his daughter Babbie and her husband, Oliver Chute. In the following year, the Chutes built a Cape-style house at 16 Bullock Lane for their summer home. The blueprints for this house were also ordered by mail from a catalog and Oliver Chute built it himself. The second floor remained unfinished until the Chutes sold the house to Richmond Hamilton, a Princeton builder, in the 1950s. The house has since come back into the Chute family and is presently owned by three of Chute's grandchildren. The Chutes summered here until the 1950s. Members of the Bullock and Chute families continue to own 16 and 26 Bullock Lane today. The association of all three of these properties on Bullock Lane with the same family adds to the historical interest of this area.

The popularity of catalog houses like those of the Chute family predates the Depression. House designs, purchased through periodicals and catalogs, grew in response to mass-marketing trends of the late nineteenth and early twentieth centuries. *Ladies' Home Journal* promoted the idea of owning a home in beautiful natural surroundings, with fresh air and light. By the end of the nineteenth century, many people wanted to live the ideal way of life that was centered on living in the country. The rising middle class had no servants and was influenced by these magazines. These smaller houses fit nicely into their lifestyles. The inexpensive plans for these houses could be altered to the needs of the buyer, and prefabricated houses could be shipped by rail to anywhere in the country. Another example of a catalog house is the 1918 Thomas Allen House at 32 Allen Hill Road, located in the Princeton Center Historic District.

As Princeton's summer resort era reached its high point between 1870 and 1915, its few industries fell into severe decline. By the time the last hotel burned in 1923, Princeton was shifting back to being an agricultural community. At the same time, the town's population fell from 1,279 year-round residents in 1870 to 707 in 1935.

RUSSELL CORNER TODAY

It is remarkable and wonderful that none of Russell Corner's houses has been demolished. Only one additional house was built. The Colonial

Revival house at 18 Sterling Road was built between 1940 and 1942 by Peter Densmore, a descendant of Charles Russell, and his wife, Anne. They hired Mr. Lahti, a Finnish shipbuilder and town resident, to hew the two exposed carrying beams in the living room of the house. The attached shop, which is post and beam construction, was built in 1946. The timbers were taken from the dilapidated barn behind the Boylston farmhouse at 73 Worcester Road. The land originally belonged to the three Walley sisters, who were also descendants of Charles Russell.

The cottage on the same property as 16 Merriam Road was built in 1949 to provide summer quarters for Ted Densmore, the eldest son of Mrs. Edward Densmore. Ted and his family of five enjoyed their little cottage for some time, and after they no longer needed it, the cottage provided temporary housing for a series of family members. Mrs. Densmore arranged for the purchase and relocation of two rectangular buildings that had been used in Concord, Massachusetts, for offices on construction sites. These were placed at right angles to each other, and a kitchen and bathroom were built into the corner. The cottage, in keeping with the other houses in Russell Corner, was named for its color and is known as the Little Red House.

Wachusett, from Russell Corner, Princeton, Mass

Wachusett Mountain, as seen from Russell Corner in the 1920s. The stone steps may have led to the former Peter Goodnow House. *Princeton Historical Society.*

Russell Corner had two major families who were seasonal residents: the Russells and the Bullocks. These families returned to Princeton for several decades of summers and both still have family members living in Russell Corner. The houses at 6, 16 and 28 Merriam Road are occupied by descendants of John Russell, as is the house at 18 Sterling Road. The houses at 16 and 26 Bullock Lane are homes of the descendants of Chandler Bullock. Their current owners continue to observe Princeton's great legacy of community involvement. Though the remaining houses have been sold to others not related to the Russell and Bullock families, they serve as gracious homes to their new residents.

Today, the Russell Corner Historic District is a quiet residential neighborhood. The visual and historic character remains intact. The economic misfortunes of the 1930s that brought a halt to commerce and development may have contributed to the fact that Russell Corner still looks like the nineteenth-century agrarian village it once was—another reason that everything is just right around Russell Corner!

CHAPTER FOUR

GREEK DRAMA IN PRINCETON

The East Princeton Story

The East Princeton Historic District was listed in the National Register of Historic Places on March 18, 2004, by the National Park Service. It encompasses about fifty-four acres and includes the village of East Princeton. The roads that compose the district include Main Street, Leominster Road, portions of Gleason Road and Beaman Road. Remnants of the long-gone mills that were the heart of East Princeton can still be seen at the foot of Gleason Road. This area, and the discontinued road that serviced it, is still known as Mill Hill by some longtime residents.

For many years, this little village within the town of Princeton was largely self-sufficient. Stores, blacksmith shops, a tavern, a school, a chapel and, later, a gasoline station all took root there. East Princeton still retains much of the character of the late nineteenth century. The charm of the Greek Revival buildings that were constructed between 1841 and 1857 still have a story to tell of days gone by, when life was much simpler.

The Greek Revival architecture that was popular in New England at this time is on prominent display here. These buildings, with their characteristic Greek Revival features, mimic the façades of Greek temples. Gable-front façades, broad eaves, friezes, gable returns and corner pilasters are found on most of the houses and barns in East Princeton. Many of the barns feature the same gable-front form as the houses, with a cart entry set to one side of the main façade and a ground-floor-level window on the other. New England ingenuity is on glorious display in the design of these barns, with window placement that serves not only to light the interior of the barn but also to lend visual balance. Several of these barns are attached to their respective houses, a common practice in New England after about 1815 and through the end of the nineteenth century. Many of the houses are tucked snugly

East Princeton is depicted in this drawing by Rosalind Sturges Allen for the fiftieth anniversary of the Princeton Historical Society. *Princeton Historical Society.*

beside their neighbors in proximity to the road. Farms that once stretched behind each house are easily visualized within the network of stone walls that now trail off into the adjacent Leominster State Forest land.

Although Greek Revival is the dominant style in East Princeton, it is not the only style. A few houses conform to the side-gabled architectural form that was common among the early settlers in the seventeenth century. Some other styles of architecture found in the village include Federal, Second Empire, Gothic Revival and a Stick-style former chapel. These styles show the change in architectural preferences and an interest in what was fashionable at the time. East Princeton had a full complement of mill owners and businessmen, and it is thanks to them that East Princeton's landscape reflects a sampling of these architectural styles.

It has been suggested that the popularity of the Greek Revival houses in East Princeton is related to the folklore of the time in which they were built. Nearly all of the gable-front Greek Revival houses in East Princeton share a feature that can be found in some, but not all, of this style throughout central Massachusetts and southern New Hampshire. It is thought that the misalignment of the first- and second-story windows on the façades of these houses can be traced to a religious movement called Millerism.

In 1818, William Miller, a devout Baptist, calculated that the world was going to end on October 22, 1844, and that Jesus would come again. In 1831, he published a book about his theory and went on a speaking tour of the Northeast. Many people doubted him, but in his enthusiasm he brought between 50,000 and 100,000 people from central and eastern Massachusetts into his fold. These people were called Millerites, and many gave up all of their belongings as they prepared for the day of the second coming. The misalignment of windows was thought to ease the believer's path to ascension.

As October 22 drew closer, a comet blazed across the Massachusetts sky, convincing these believers that the end was coming. The Millerites dressed in white robes and climbed mountains or trees to bring themselves closer

According to folklore, Greek Revival houses, similar to the one at 80 Main Street in East Princeton, are known as Ascension Houses. *Princeton Historical Society*.

to their ascension into heaven. Wachusett Mountain, the highest elevation in central Massachusetts, was a logical place for them to gather. When the prophecy did not come to pass, most of the Millerites returned to their former religions.

It is not known if the residents of East Princeton were followers of William Miller. Some of the houses bearing the characteristic window arrangement were built after the prophetic date of October 22, 1844, calling into question a direct link between the architecture and Millerism. The possibility of this association, however, continues to intrigue people who fondly refer to these homes as Ascension Houses.

EARLY SETTLERS AND NEW BEGINNINGS

It is difficult to determine when the earliest settlers arrived in Princeton because many owned land for years before actually settling on it, while others may have occupied the land before actually recording the deed. Princeton history tells that Joshua Wilder is known to have been the first settler to come westward from Lancaster, Massachusetts, and establish his home on the outskirts of East Princeton, along the Bay Path. The path then traveled to Sterling Road, up Merriam Road and west to Mountain Road, where it went in a southerly direction to Worcester Road. As time passed, this roadway was transformed from its original footpath into the modern roads of today.

Joshua was son of Nathaniel Wilder, of Lancaster, and grandson of the elder Nathaniel, who was killed in one of the Indian attacks in Lancaster. Joshua Wilder was born in Lancaster on September 20, 1712. In 1743, the same year that his father moved from Lancaster to Petersham, Wilder settled his family in Princeton. The year before, he petitioned the General Court of the Massachusetts Bay Colony for land and was granted 120 acres. The following is part of the petition that Wilder made to the court:

> *That your Petitioner Tho a Poor man yet he humbly apprehends he has the Character of an Honest and Laboureous man and is minded to settle himself & family thereon.*
>
> *That therefore he is desirous of obtaining a Grant of said land on such condition as may be consistent with your Excellency & Hon Wisdom & on as Easy terms as may be, and should he obtain it he apprehends it would be of great service to People Travelling from Lancaster to the new towns now Settleing westward to have a house to resort to in their Travaling.*

Your Petitioner therefore humbly prays your Excellency and Hon to take ye premises into your wise consideration and act thereon as may be consistent with your known Goodness & your petitioner shall as in duty bound ever pray etc.

For Wilder, the following reply from the statehouse set the wheels in motion for a new and adventurous life for him, his wife, Sarah, and their three children:

Upon this petition, the General Court, April 7th, 1743, ordered that the land be granted, provided the petitioner does within one year have a good and convenient house built thereon for the accommodation of Travellers, and have ten acres thereof cleared, and brought to English grass or plowing within four years, and that he dwell thereon with his family, or have one other good family dwell thereon.

The court was wise to have granted land to Joshua Wilder in the hopes of encouraging new settlements. He consciously honored the pact that he made with the government and within the year established a "good and convenient house built for the reception of both Man or Beast." Wilder remained in Princeton until about 1755, when he lost his property over a business speculation on cattle that he supplied to the army in Canada. He sold his house and land and moved to Ware, Massachusetts, with his large family. He died there in 1762.

It is difficult to imagine what he must have experienced as he traveled to this unknown territory. Simple hatchet marks on trees may have helped him mark his way as he moved along on horseback. The trail was narrow and danger lurked at every turn. Wilder chose a suitable location for his house/tavern on a route that would soon be frequently traveled by others. The house was located on a slight elevation not far from a stream. For Joshua Wilder and his family of eleven children, the tavern was his link to the outside world. People traveling from Lancaster and points east stopped for lodging or a bit of refreshment as they brought news of family and friends from the towns they left behind.

For a time, there were no neighbors for the Wilders. Joshua's task of farming his land, keeping his tavern and caring for his family was all he could manage. However, as time went on more people came to Princeton, and by 1761 there were about forty-two families living there. The site where his house once stood is near the intersection of Houghton and Bullard Roads, on what is now the Norco Sportsman's Club property, just outside the southern boundary of the current East Princeton Historical District. Scattered stones from a foundation are the only indication that this man lived there.

John Keyes is the earliest settler to be identified with the development of the village of East Princeton. John, a distant cousin of Princeton pioneer Robert Keyes, was born in 1753 in the nearby town of Boylston. He married Lucy Hale and lived in Wilton, New Hampshire, with their two sons before settling in Princeton in 1781. John purchased 550 acres in East Princeton. His house, which is no longer standing, is thought to have been located in the vicinity of 80 Main Street. He purchased a saw- and gristmill from a man named Martin and established his business along a brook (later known as Keyes Brook). He was joined by his brother, Ephraim, and as the village began to grow, other families moved to East Princeton. John and Lucy eventually had nine children, and their descendants remained in East Princeton, engaged in trades similar to those of their ancestors.

Most New England towns had a tavern and East Princeton was no exception. The tavern was centrally located on Main Street and is mentioned in an 1851 deed for a piece of property across the street from where the building is now located. The deed states that the land on the northwest corner of Main Street and Leominster Road had been part of the "old Tavern farm" and that "the public house recently thereon" had been kept by "Amos Keyes." It is possible that John, the father of Amos, may have run the tavern, but there is no mention of any earlier tavern keepers. The phrase "public house recently thereon" suggests that the tavern had recently been moved off that land. It seems likely that Amos Keyes's tavern was moved across the street to 67 Main Street and may also have been known as the Cotton Tavern at one time. This Federal-style, hip-roofed building is the only one of this style in East Princeton, and it is understandable how it may have achieved the status of tavern based on its size.

Taverns were important in rural communities in the eighteenth and nineteenth centuries. As was the case with Joshua Wilder and his tavern, Keyes's tavern served the same purpose of sharing and passing news among neighbors. The only public gathering places in small villages, taverns were the setting for local politics. It may be that this was one of the first commercial establishments to operate in East Princeton. Locally, as well as elsewhere in New England, the tavern may have sold supplies on a small scale to residents and visitors alike. The building has since been converted into apartments.

In 1830, there were very few houses located in this area, and most were farms, scattered some distance apart. At the turn of the twentieth century, Princeton historian Francis Blake published an overlay of the 1830 Amos

Ephraim Keyes's house (35 Leominster Road) is believed to be the earliest house in the village. It remained in the Keyes family until 1931. *Princeton Historical Society.*

Merriam map. On the map he showed houses that were standing at the time the 1830 map was drawn. There were possibly as many as six houses and a school in East Princeton. The Keyes brothers owned two of the houses. Ephraim, who settled here in the late eighteenth century, lived in the house at 35 Leominster Road. The history of this Federal-style Cape house dates back to the late 1700s, when it was built by Keyes about the time of his marriage, in 1790, to Sally Geary of Boylston. It is believed to be the oldest house in East Princeton. The house was passed down to Silas, one of the nine Keyes children, and remained in the family for three generations until 1931.

Daniel Baker and his son-in-law, Orange Welch, lived at opposite ends of Main Street. The northern end of the street was more populous, and it was in this area that Daniel and Orange ran a blacksmith shop. Baker appears to have been living here in the early 1800s. It is likely that they were the first blacksmiths in the village, and Daniel continued in the blacksmith trade until sometime after 1851. He died at the age of ninety-eight. Baker's daughter Lorinda and her husband, Orange, lived in the vicinity of 38 Main Street, the last house at the southern end of the district. During the time that Baker lived in East Princeton, his skills as a blacksmith were indispensible. His jobs included repairing tools and wagons and shoeing

75

Leominster Road was once a tree-lined dirt road with sidewalks. The East Princeton fire barn is seen at the far left. *Nancy Hubbard.*

horses. Once the mills started operating, there was more work for him as the community grew.

The houses of Elisha Hager and James Brown were located on the west side of Main Street at the northern end, near Keyes Brook, where Brown had his mill. The District Three Schoolhouse was located at the intersection of Beaman Road and Route 140.

The Amos Merriam map shows Main Street running through the village, and as early as 1851, it was designated a county road. Leominster Road may have served in the late eighteenth and early nineteenth centuries as a local route between the farms of the brothers John and Ephraim Keyes. This map linked the Stuart mill in Sterling with their mill in East Princeton. Gleason Road is not shown on the 1830 map but was described in 1832 as the road leading from John Keyes's place to James Brown's. James Brown Sr. owned a farm, which is standing today at 72 Gleason Road, just outside the district. Route 31, at the northern end of the district, was not constructed until 1871 and is shown only as a dotted line in the 1870 atlas of Worcester County. Keyes Brook passed under Main Street, where a bridge traversed the stream. In the early days, travel through the village was on narrow dusty roads. In the winter, the roads were shoveled by hand or cleared with a snow roller pulled by a team of horses or oxen. Spring travel was hampered by mud.

THE STREAM THAT MADE A VILLAGE

The landscape of America at the time of the Revolution was mostly agricultural. The New England landscape was composed of a scattering of small villages set among pastures and fields carved out of the forest. Here and there a gristmill or sawmill was built along a stream. These were family-owned industries in which the mill owners and employees serviced a local economy by grinding grain, forging tools and milling lumber. Mill villages often appear picturesque and inviting in scenes drawn as reminders of the old days. It is easy to forget that the purpose of these mills was to produce goods in the most efficient and economical way. Children worked in the mills, as well as adults, and sometimes for as many as ten to twelve hours a day in less than favorable conditions. In 1880, there was a mill in East Princeton that had fifteen male hands, and three of them were younger than fifteen. The mills were hot in the summer and cold in the winter, but production goals, despite the weather, had to be met. There were no safety regulations and there were frequent accidents.

East Princeton's development is the story of a stream that made a village. It wasn't until the 1840s that the first water-powered chair factories were established on Keyes Brook. These factories, clustered at the foot of Mill Hill, eventually made East Princeton a major center for chair manufacturing in New England. They remained an important part of Princeton's economy for nearly seventy years.

The beginning of industrial development during the 1840s and '50s defined many New England towns, including East Princeton. While eighteenth-century communities were established around a common as the center of activity, such as Princeton Center, nineteenth-century towns were often built along streams. Keyes Brook, a swift stream with cascading waters, was an ideal place to establish a mill. Given the hilly terrain in this area, it was logical to use its swift streams for water-powered industries. Princeton's rocky soil supports abundant forests that supplied hardwood for its sawmills and chair factories. The soil also provided local stone for the sluiceways, bridges and footings. The downside of these virtues was that the mills were limited by the water power capacity, which ceased in summer droughts. The lack of a direct rail route through East Princeton further limited growth.

Farmers looking for a way to supplement their earnings made chairs by hand during the eighteenth and early nineteenth centuries. Woodworking industries in northern Worcester County towns soon flourished. By the early nineteenth century, chair-making shops had been established in almost every town in the county. By 1820, the nearby town of Sterling was the chair-making center of the region, with a yearly production of 70,000 chairs. East Princeton, in 1832, had two chair makers. One of these was an artisan chair maker who, with only two helpers, produced 1,500 rocking chairs a year—some were made of mahogany. The other chair manufacturer had five helpers and made 10,500 "common chairs" of pine, oak and maple. Elsewhere in Princeton, there was one manufacturer of cotton shirting, two tanners, one manufacturer of boots and shoes and one maker of palm leaf hats and straw braid.

East Princeton can date its change from a rural settlement to an industrial village to the middle years of the nineteenth century, when the chair-making industry began to take hold. The year 1857 saw as many as four chair shops and one sawmill operating in the village.

HAVE A SEAT: EAST PRINCETON CHAIR MAKERS

The chair-making industry in East Princeton can be credited to a few families, starting with the arrival of the Stuarts and the Browns. Benjamin Stuart Jr. was born in 1793 and was an experienced chair manufacturer in the town of Sterling on Justice Hill, near the Princeton town line. His son Joseph joined him in the chair-making business, and to meet competition, they expanded when Joseph bought John Keyes's water power site on Keyes Brook in 1841. The Stuart factory in Sterling probably supplied Joseph and his father with the raw materials they needed for the assembly of their chairs in East Princeton. Soon after the Stuarts began making chairs, additional chair factories, and a sawmill, began operating nearby.

Joseph Stuart was born in 1815, and at the age of thirty-five he established the Joseph M. Stuart Co. in East Princeton. In 1850, he was producing over twenty thousand chairs per year, with twelve people employed in his factory. As Joseph's business grew, he purchased a house on a twelve-acre portion of the Old Tavern Farm land. The impressively large Greek Revival house at 70 Main Street is testament to Joseph's importance in the village as a mill owner. Considering the large size of the house, it seems possible that some of Joseph's employees may have boarded there. Joseph sold his property, including the 70 Main Street home, to his younger brother, John, in January 1860. This house and several others in East Princeton were built by Edson Beaman, a well-known Princeton blacksmith who was also an active local builder.

By the 1850s John Stuart had joined the chair-making business with his father and brother, and the company was known as Benjamin Stuart and Sons. Sometime before 1870, John took over both the East Princeton chair-making business and the sawmill in Sterling. By 1880, the company was producing chairs and furniture valued at $30,000 a year. After John's death, his son Arthur L. succeeded him, and the firm became known as the A.L. Stuart Company.

James and Abigail Brown came to Princeton from Sterling in 1791 and settled just outside East Princeton Village in the house at 72 Gleason Road. Starting in the 1840s, their son James operated a chair factory at the northern end of Main Street, just a short distance from the Stuart mill. It is not known for certain when James started manufacturing chairs. It may be that he was already an experienced chair maker in Sterling before coming to Princeton.

William Brown joined his father, James, as a partner in the chair-making business in 1849. In 1850, they had eighteen men producing thirty thousand chairs per year, valued at $15,000. By 1860, their chair production had increased to fifty thousand, with sixteen men in their employ. The value of these chairs in 1860 was $16,500. Brown's business did well until 1861, when fire destroyed the factory and an adjoining grocery store. William Brown became sole owner of the business and rebuilt the factory. The company closed permanently after the last fire destroyed the mill again in 1877.

The former Brown chair factory at 93 Main Street may have housed the office and store downstairs and the factory upstairs. The attached barn may have been used to store wagonloads of chairs until they were ready to be taken to Sterling for rail shipment. Although all of the manufacturing buildings are gone, many of the properties that Brown owned are still a part of the village. Across Main Street from the former factory are three small Greek Revival houses that Brown built for his factory workers. They are located at 96, 98 and 100 Main Street and stand as a testament to how people in East Princeton lived and worked in proximity. All of the mill owners in the village provided housing for their employees, and it was common for the workers to live in the same house as, or near, their employers. Brown, whose business dominated the northern end of Main Street, did not live far from his factory. His Greek Revival home at 85 Main Street was a short distance from his mill office and his other properties. By 1898, Brown's house was owned by Arthur L. Stuart. At one time in the late nineteenth century, the house had an open Queen Anne wraparound porch. During this period, architectural fashion dictated the trend toward porches, with an emphasis on gardens and outdoor spaces. In the late twentieth century, as traffic increased, the porch was enclosed.

On the east side of Gleason Road, Mark Wilder operated a sawmill along Keyes Brook as early as 1847. He employed four men who milled chestnut and pine. The sawmill was a lucrative business for Wilder as the population grew in the village. Native trees were cut and brought to the mill, where they were turned into lumber for the new houses in East Princeton. The Wilder mill is believed to have been the largest of all the nearby mills in East Princeton at the time. A building labeled Saw & Turning Mills is seen straddling the brook in the 1870 atlas. Wilder remained in operation until sometime around 1879, when Charles W. Reed and Foster E. Matthews purchased his sawmill. Fire destroyed all of the factory buildings and a house in 1899.

A short time later, Foster Matthews sold his part in the mill to John H. Temple and the name was changed to Reed & Temple. In 1894, Temple bought Reed's portion of Reed & Temple and formed a partnership with Benjamin Stuart of New York City. The two men improved their chair factory with the addition of a paint shop, where chairs were dipped into large varnish vats. This process brought a new era in chair finishing to the industry. A second fire at this site destroyed the buildings that had replaced the earlier ones. The buildings were never rebuilt after the second fire.

As the chair industry prospered, other small businesses were established to support the manufacturing effort and the needs of the workers. Amos Keyes

A new method of applying varnish was employed by the Temple-Stuart Paint Shop, where chairs were dipped into large vats of varnish. *Nancy Hubbard.*

and his son Ezra had workshops across from their homes at the south end of Main Street. Amos lived at 46 Main Street, and Ezra's house, the last in the district, was at 38 Main Street. These two businesses appeared as early as 1857. According to early maps, the two shops did not appear to be located near Keyes Brook, suggesting that much of the work was done by hand. Amos Keyes manufactured chairs and furniture with a capital investment of $1,000 and employed six male workers. An 1881 brochure for Princeton businesses shows that his company was making parlor brackets, toys and novelties in woodenware. By 1898, Ezra's son Atwood was carrying on the business of wheelwright, carriage painter and photographer. His work was described as "general jobbing and new work." The brochure listed him as a carriage painter with "special attention to repairing and jobbing." He also

16 ADVERTISEMENTS.

DR. O. HOWE, DENTIST,

PRINCETON, - - MASS.

Teeth Filled with Gold, Silver, Amalgam or Cement.

ARTIFICIAL TEETH skilfully inserted on all of the bases used by the profession. Ether administered when desired.

PRICES REASONABLE AND WORK FIRST-CLASS.

Visits Westminster and Hubbardston once in two weeks.

A. H. KEYES & SON,

MANUFACTURERS OF

PARLOR BRACKETS, TOYS,

—AND—

Novelties in Wooden Ware,

EAST PRINCETON, MASS.

A. B. KEYES,

EAST PRINCETON,

Wheelwright and Carriage Painter.

Special attention given to General Repairing and Jobbing.

Stereoscopic Views taken of Dwellings and Public Buildings. Photography in all its branches.

In 1881, Atwood Keyes and Amos Keyes, as well as J.H. Stuart, advertized their manufacturing businesses in the Princeton Business Directory. *Princeton Historical Society.*

offered "photography in all its branches" and "Stereoscopic Views taken of Dwellings and Public Buildings." John Keyes, East Princeton's earliest settler, had established his name in the village and, through successive generations, left a sense of family pride and a place in history here.

In 1857, there was one blacksmith shop located at the south end of Main Street near Mill Hill. By 1870, there were two blacksmith shops, one operated by J.P. Wood and the other by James C. Coburn at 90 Main Street. In addition to maintaining farm machinery, the Wood and Coburn shops depended on nearby mills for much of their business, and, in turn, the mills required the blacksmith shop to keep their equipment in working order. The shops of both Coburn and Wood were located nearly opposite the mills.

During the nineteenth century, it was not unusual for manufacturing companies to cover all or part of the cost of fire protection in the vicinity of their mills. Fire protection was improved in 1892 when money was appropriated at town meeting for two horse-drawn pumper trucks. One truck was housed in Princeton Center and the other was kept in a small building on Temple's property at the corner of Leominster Road and Main Street. Temple's family operated the Temple-Lamson Store on this same property, which may have linked the ownership of the firehouse and the pumper truck to John Temple. As the fire trucks increased in size, this building became small and outdated. The trucks were later garaged at Hubbard's Garage at 106 Main Street.

It is not clear when the first store opened in East Princeton. There may have been a small store operating in the tavern, or perhaps in conjunction with the Keyes mill, sometime around 1841. East Princeton's first known store was the Union Store, at 85 Main Street. It opened in 1848 and was probably operated by John A. Mirick. Warren Whitcomb became the proprietor in 1885 and continued until 1921. The name of the store was changed to East Princeton Country Store when Clayton Cadwell operated it in the 1950s and '60s. During both Whitcomb's and Cadwell's proprietorship, the East Princeton Post Office was located in this store. It remained there until 1984, when it closed and merged with the Princeton Post Office in the Gregory Hill Store near the center of Princeton. While the post office remained in East Princeton, it maintained its own zip code of 01571. Marjorie Bingham, a former resident, remembered the store being open until eleven o'clock at night during the Second World War. This was a time when people had victory gardens and bought their canning supplies at the store.

The Temple-Lamson Store was located at 66 Main Street. It was built in 1851 and was run in partnership by the husbands of John Stuart's daughters, Janie and Marion. It is supposed that one or both of the men

East Princeton's Union Store and East Princeton Post Office, located in the store, opened in 1848 and continued in business until the early 1980s. *Nancy Hubbard*.

Clayton Cadwell, proprietor of the East Princeton Country Store during the 1950s and '60s, is shown helping a customer. *Princeton Historical Society*.

may have managed the store for Stuart and later took over ownership. It remained in business until around 1941. The store was one of three buildings located on this property. The Gothic Revival house at the southern end may have been built to accommodate employees of the Stuart factory or storekeepers of the adjoining company store. It is unique in its details, which include Corinthian-style capitals on the front porch posts. This is the only Gothic Revival house in the district. The large barn served as an overnight depot for wagonloads of chairs that were taken each day to the railroad. The barn has one large sliding door to the right through which the wagons entered. Loaded with chairs and settees, they were stored in preparation for the trip to the railroad station. Another door, located to the left, was the entrance to the part of the barn where the horses were kept. A large, wooden, cross-gabled cupola is located in the center of the barn roof. This block of buildings, which now serves as apartments, is still a visible reminder of the days when the chair factories were operating. The house retains its name, the Beehive, which referred to the flurry of activity associated with the chair makers.

Not all activity in East Princeton was commercial. Gamaliel Beaman, an American Impressionist painter, lived in the house at 85 Main Street in the 1920s. Beaman, born in 1852, studied at the Art Institute in Lowell, Massachusetts, and in Paris. He was a member of the Boston Art Club

Following a day of chair making, the Temple-Stuart chair team is ready for delivery of the settees and chairs to the railroad in Sterling. *Nancy Hubbard.*

and specialized in oil paintings and watercolors of landscapes, still lifes and flowers. Before his death in 1937, he had established a fine reputation as an artist. His paintings can be seen today in several private Princeton collections, as well as at the Princeton Public Library, the Princeton Historical Society and throughout the United States. Beaman became interested in antiques and sold them as a means to augment the sale of his artwork, earning him the nickname "Antique Beaman."

THE GOOD LIFE IN THE VILLAGE

With the beginning of the chair industry in 1841, East Princeton transformed from a rural community into a bustling village. The success of the mills led to the growth of the village. New house construction and the opening of businesses served an ever-increasing population. The district school, which originally served a neighborhood of dispersed farmsteads, was enlarged and moved closer to the village center. By 1857, the settlement grew from a few dwellings to include as many as thirteen homes, a number of shops, three water-powered mills and a combined school and function hall.

In March 1852, to accommodate the growing population in East Princeton, the Town of Princeton elected a three-person committee to "determine the condition of District Three School and report as to the expense of repairing or replacing the building then standing" at the intersection of Beaman Road and what is now Route 140. A town meeting in April 1852 voted to give District Three the sum of $525, as well as the lumber from the old school to build a new one. The new building, whose architect is unknown, had two classrooms downstairs and a meeting hall upstairs. The final cost, including the materials from the old school, was $600. School was held in the two first-floor classrooms for nearly ninety years.

The new East Princeton school building, also known as Mechanics Hall, outshone the other nine district schools in Princeton in both size and design. It was built in the Greek Revival style, with a projecting pedimented façade supported by four fluted Doric columns. Its size and architectural beauty made it a prominent focal point in the village, and the building remained the village center for many years. It remained in use as a school until 1945. It was the last district school in Princeton to close.

The building served the village not only as a school but also as a meeting place and community hall. Organizations such as the Princeton Farmers Club, which by 1882 had become the Princeton Farmers and Mechanics

Mechanics Hall was the heart of the village and served as a school and meeting hall from 1852 until the 1980s. *Princeton Historical Society.*

Association, held meetings and lectures here. It was at this time that the building became known as Mechanics Hall.

Although Mechanics Hall was built in 1852, it is interesting to note that the date 1843 appears on the pediment. The reason for this is unknown, but it may have been intended to show the date of the former schoolhouse, from which lumber was used for this building.

Another organization that was active in East Princeton was the East Princeton Village Improvement Society. This group was founded in the late nineteenth century by the wives of the factory and store owners. These dedicated women were instrumental in establishing sidewalks and gas streetlights that extended from Leominster Road to Beaman Road.

At a town meeting held in 1903, the town voted that the sum of $300 be raised and appropriated for establishing and maintaining streetlights in the residential districts of Princeton Center and East Princeton. Arrangements were made with the Globe Gaslight Company, and nearly one hundred lights were provided—twenty-five for the village. Eventually, electric lights replaced the gas lamps. Edith Hubbard, a former East Princeton resident, spoke of Mr. Anderson, who lived at the southern end of Main Street:

He would come around four o'clock each afternoon and light the street lamps. The next morning he would return and extinguish them, and bring the globes home to be cleaned. Each day he repeated his task.

The society held dances and suppers in Mechanics Hall to raise funds for sidewalk maintenance and other amenities in the village. A bandstand was built in front of the big barn at 66 Main Street. It was said to have been painted yellow with a white fence around it. Princeton's own Cornet Band frequently held concerts there.

It was during this whirl of social and civic activity that members of the Congregational Church petitioned their minister, Reverend Archibald Love, to build a chapel in East Princeton. In 1885, William Brown, former chair manufacturer, and his wife sold the land for the chapel for a penny. The deed was made out to Reverend Love. Princeton residents contributed money for the chapel, and construction was carried out with the help of local people under the direction of builder John C.F. Mirick. During the early part of the twentieth century, the minister traveled each Sunday from Princeton Center to the chapel, where he conducted services at three o'clock. For many years, the church was an active and important

The Stick-style chapel in the village was host to a variety of activities that served the community from 1885 until it closed in 1960. *Nancy Hubbard.*

part of the community. The Ladies Aid Society held suppers there once a month.

The chapel was designed in the then fashionable Stick-style architecture and is the only example of this style in East Princeton. Now a private residence, the chapel still retains its architectural integrity, including bands of decorative shingling, a bell tower with the original bell and simple, two-color stained-glass windows in the upper sashes.

The chapel had the misfortune of being just outside the range of a significant village amenity. Residents along Leominster Road and a portion of Main Street enjoyed the convenience of running water, pumped into their homes from a cistern. The cistern was fed by a spring at the foot of Gleason Road. Pipes were laid only as far as 11 Leominster Road and stopped before the chapel. Maintenance of the water pipe was the responsibility of homeowners fortunate enough to have access to running water. These residents were charged a fee collected by the person living at 66 Main Street. Remnants of this early system can still be found.

This system included a stone watering trough at the intersection of Main Street and Gleason Road. Horses pulling their wagonloads of chairs and settees up the steep hills of Gleason Road or up south Main Street would stop there for a drink of water. The trough now functions as a flower planter and remains a landmark.

A VILLAGE IN TRANSITION

The early twentieth century brought major changes to East Princeton. The two remaining chair factories, A.L. Stuart Co. and the Temple Company, merged in 1904 to form the Temple-Stuart Company. Six years later, the factory suffered a devastating fire and nearly all of its buildings were destroyed. The factory was not rebuilt. By this time, electricity and steam power had replaced the water wheels, and these newer power sources freed manufacturing from river sites. The Temple-Stuart Company relocated to a twenty-three-acre site in Baldwinville, Massachusetts. After seventy years, chair production in East Princeton had drawn to a close.

With the loss of its largest employer, the population within the village decreased dramatically. Princeton resident Jeanette Sullivan, who attended school at Mechanics Hall in 1919, recalls that at that time there was only one class with eight or nine children, including a few from Sterling. Jeanette also recalls a well in front of Mechanics Hall from which the children drank. At the age of twenty, Jeanette herself was teaching school in Princeton.

Roland Keyes is seen in his automobile outside the former Temple-Stuart storage barn, where he had an automotive shop. *Nancy Hubbard.*

Another source of change was the advent of the automobile. Cars offered increased mobility, giving residents the freedom to look beyond their village for employment and recreation. Commerce in the village began to center on this new arrival. To meet the needs of automobile traffic, two gasoline filling stations and an automobile paint shop opened in the village. In 1907, Roland Keyes purchased the only surviving Temple-Stuart building, located at the intersection of Gleason Road and Main Street. This building was originally a barn belonging to the property at 77 Main Street, which was later used by the Temple-Stuart Company for storage. Roland Keyes transformed the storage barn into an automobile paint shop, where he painted and pinstriped automobiles and sold auto accessories. The paint shop was converted into a house sometime in the 1950s.

Around 1928, the Slongwhites built a Shell gas station at the intersection of Route 140 and Beaman Road, where the two early district schoolhouses once stood. The sign over the front porch advertised hot dogs, tobacco, cigars, cold tonic, candy and sandwiches. By 1931, a new sign appeared that read, "White House Retreat, Come and See Us." The small, gable-front, clapboarded office with gasoline pumps out front was enlarged in the 1930s or 1940s.

As the automobile became popular, the Slongwhites' Shell gas station opened as a roadside retreat offering candy, sandwiches and hot dogs, as well as gasoline. Route 140 is seen to the right. *Donald Slongwhite.*

The other filling station was Hubbard's Garage, where John and Charles Hubbard repaired automobiles, sold gasoline and housed the fire trucks.

Despite the loss of the chair industry once central to East Princeton, the village remained an active community. The East Princeton Village Improvement Society continued to hold functions, though on a smaller scale. After the suppers were discontinued, the society held parties for the children, a tradition that continued until the 1980s. New organizations formed as well, including American Legion Post 334. In addition to hosting the legion, Mechanics Hall also served as a branch library. Norma Passage, who lived on the other side of town on Old Colony Road, served as librarian during the 1960s.

The East Princeton chapel, however, did fall victim to the changing times. When Reverend Love moved from Princeton to Connecticut, he deeded the East Princeton chapel property to the Home Missionary Society. In 1945, the title was transferred to the First Congregational Church of Princeton. At an annual meeting in 1960, the congregation voted to discontinue services. In the 1970s, the chapel was sold and has since been restored as a private residence.

Change also befell the long-departed Temple-Stuart Company. In 1990, the company closed the door to its Baldwinville factory. Its assets were acquired by Roxton Furniture, a Canadian company. Roxton Temple-Stuart Ltd. continued making furniture in Waterloo, Ontario, at least until 2003.

Clayton Hubbard, whose ancestors settled Princeton, ran the family dairy farm all his life and later passed it down to his son, Arthur, and grandson, Bradford. *Nancy Hubbard.*

With the exception of the factories that are no longer standing, East Princeton's landscape has changed very little. The fires that summoned the end of the chair-making era took very few houses. Nearly all of the original houses remain, keeping the nineteenth-century feel of the area intact, in spite of the challenges of heavy traffic on the former County Road (Route 140) through East Princeton.

Today's residents still enjoy many conveniences of village life. An automotive repair shop, store and eatery are all within walking distance and are all located in historic buildings. Sawyer Park, established in 1979, provides a place for the neighborhood children to play and is a small oasis in the high-traffic environment that surrounds it. Today, Keyes Brook is surrounded by Department of Conservation and Recreation land. The waterway that once brought industry to the village now provides an unspoiled wooded sanctuary.

Some agriculture remains in the village on residential farms and in extensive gardens, maple syrup collections and bee-keeping enterprises. Keyes Brook flows freely past the mill sites that once harnessed its energy and continues to serve East Princeton as a rural fire hydrant.

The massive stone footings laid by men and oxen still support the bridge on Gleason Road. Standing here today it is easy to imagine how it was, many years ago, when the mills were running. Looking north, the stone footings that supported the mills are visible, as well as the wheel pit for the overshot wheel at the Brown Mill. The massive stones, through which the water ran its course in a southerly direction, still remain as they were 150 years ago. The trees have grown and the thicket is dense, yet the beauty of Keyes Brook remains.

CHAPTER FIVE

HOW THE WEST WAS WON

The West Village Story

The West Village Historic District lies just west of Princeton Center. Settled in the mid-eighteenth century, West Village evolved as a community separate from the town center, which had developed earlier. Some of the oldest homes in Princeton are located in West Village, including one that housed Princeton's first school and another that was home to one of the town's first stores. West Village spans 465 acres in the area of Hubbardston, Goodnow, Allen Hill and Radford Roads.

Like most of Princeton, West Village began as a farming community. While other villages in town took advantage of available water power to establish grist- and sawmills, West Village had none. West Village was not, however, without commercial activity. By the early nineteenth century, West Village was home to a tavern, a stagecoach stop, a blacksmith, a wheelwright and a shoe factory. At that time, a new road system in West Village brought greater access and increased commercial development. The coming of the railway to Princeton also brought increased activity to West Village. Stagecoaches traveling from Princeton Depot to points east would stop first at West Village. By the mid-nineteenth century, West Village had become a bustling crossroads. The area continued to prosper during Princeton's summer resort era from the mid-nineteenth to the early twentieth century.

Although most of Princeton's large hotels were located near the town common, West Village had one large hotel of its own, as well as many inns. The summer resort era was a time of prosperity for West Village farmers, who provided meat, produce and other products to Princeton's thriving hotel industry.

As West Village evolved so too did its name. The village was known for a long time as "Methody Corners" for the Methodist community and

A carriage heads west down Hubbardston Road past Pratt's Annex and some young visitors. *Princeton Historical Society.*

its church, which stood at the intersection of Hubbardston, Radford and Allen Hill Roads. Later, the village became known as "Pratt's Corners," for the Pratt family, who operated several inns at the same intersection. West Village was also known for a time as "Lower Village" to distinguish it from Princeton Center. It was also once known as "Other Hill." The name West Village continued well into the twentieth century, long after the loss of the Methodist Church to fire and the closing of the inns.

In its earliest days, West Village was no more than a school and a few farmsteads along Hubbardston Road. This small cluster of buildings was connected to the early town center by a road that led from the meetinghouse to the southwest part of town. This road, known as the "Old Road to Meeting House Hill," began at what is now Mountain Road and followed the dirt path just south of Meeting House Cemetery. Today, this path trails off onto private land, but in the past the route continued down the lower part of Allen Hill Road, where it followed Hubbardston Road to the end of Calamint Hill Road South.

Princeton's first school was established in one of West Village's earliest houses. In 1764, Samuel Woods became the first public schoolteacher in town, holding classes in his 136 Hubbardston Road home. With a total school budget of six pounds, Samuel Woods opened his home as Princeton's first

A stone wall leads the eye to West Village and the steeple of the former Methodist Church. *Princeton Historical Society*.

official school. Two years later, the town was divided into five school districts (North, East, Centre, West and South). This home hosted the Centre School until a schoolhouse was constructed in 1774 on Meeting House Hill. That same year, Woods was chosen as one of seven men to serve on the town's committee of correspondence to share intelligence during the Revolutionary War with other towns in the area.

When word reached Princeton that a band of the king's troops had raided the Charlestown Arsenal and was headed up the Mystic River, Princeton residents spent the night making preparations for battle, including molding pewter plates into musket bullets. Woods's son Samuel Jr. was one of many Princeton men to respond to the Lexington Alarm on April 19, 1775. Samuel Woods Sr. was highly regarded as a skillful and successful teacher for fifty years. He also served as selectman, constable and town assessor.

The earliest house in West Village was built around 1757 by a member of the Gleason family. This Cape Cod–style cottage at 68 Hubbardston Road was the site of West Village's first wheelwright shop and later its first butchery. The west section of the house was added in the 1790s, when another building (built in 1760) was moved to this site. Historic postcards refer to this house as the oldest in Princeton. While not actually the oldest house in Princeton, it is the oldest house in West Village.

Within a few years of building his home, schoolmaster Samuel Woods opened his doors to Princeton's first school. *Princeton Historical Society*.

Nestled behind towering elms and a fieldstone wall stands the Gleason House, known to be the oldest house in West Village. *Princeton Historical Society*.

West Village boasts other early houses. The property now known as the Smith Farm at 110 Hubbardston Road includes a house that was built around 1780. This house was built for Bartholomew Cheever, a lieutenant who served in the Revolutionary War. The house is thought to have originated as a smaller building than the large, two-and-a-half-story home it is today. In 1789, Dr. Ephraim Wilson, one of Princeton's earliest physicians, built a large house at 48 Hubbardston Road. Dr. Wilson ran West Village's first store from this home.

As these early houses were being constructed, so too was Goodnow Road, running from Hubbardston Road to the Goodnow family homestead. Goodnow Road would later become a major route, bringing travelers from Barre and beyond. The main road through West Village at this time was the Old Road to Meeting House Hill. It was on this road that Silas Fay Jr. built his 20 Allen Hill Road home in 1804. Fay was a cabinetmaker, and it is likely that many of the home's features, such as the leaded fanlight and pilasters surrounding the front entry, were created by Fay himself.

Road construction continued in West Village in 1807 with the addition of Radford Road. To fully appreciate the impact of Radford Road, consider that Boylston Avenue (which connects Brooks Station Road to today's town center) was not yet in existence. Radford Road became part of the main route from Princeton to Rutland and was known throughout most of the

Silas Fay Jr.'s cabinetry skills are evident in his home, including the elaborate door surround with a fanlight above. *Princeton Historical Society.*

nineteenth century as the "Road to Rutland." Hubbardston Road was extended a half mile from its intersection with Radford Road to the County Road, now Mountain and Worcester Roads. These new roads provided improved access for horses, carriages and wagons, and before long West Village was a busy crossroads.

TAVERN DAYS: TIRED, THIRSTY TRAVELERS

An increase in traffic was not the only factor in the growth of the village. The population of Princeton and the whole region was also growing. Princeton's population grew from 700 residents during the Revolutionary War years to 1,062 in 1810. That year, Schoolhouse No. 9 was established in West Village at 36 Hubbardston Road. It was one of the first buildings to be built on the new half-mile section of Hubbardston Road.

In 1814, Captain Calvin Bullock built a large, Federal-style house on this new section of Hubbardston Road. He ran a store called Bullock's Stand from his 44 Hubbardston Road home and it became a popular destination for travelers. A few years later, Peter Richardson purchased the house and continued to operate Bullock's Stand for about ten more years. Mr. Richardson also acquired Dr. Wilson's house at 48 Hubbardston Road, from which he operated a roadside tavern. The house also served as a stagecoach stop, an inn with overnight accommodations and a gathering place for assemblies, meetings and parties.

In 1824, a turnpike opened between the center of Barre and Princeton's Goodnow Road. The turnpike was an eleven-mile toll road that eliminated the six meandering, hilly miles of the former route that passed north and then west of Princeton Center. This new turnpike allowed access for a new regional stagecoach route. This was the second stage line through Princeton. The first stage line, which had started just a few years earlier in 1820, followed a north–south route through the center of town. This new line ran east–west, following Hubbardston Road, with a stop at Peter Richardson's tavern and store, up Goodnow Road and on to the western part of the state.

The rise in stagecoach travel brought steady business to wheelwright Charles Harrington. Harrington built his house at 46 Hubbardston Road, where he operated a large wheelwright shop. The size of the building suggests that Harrington's business included the production of wheels in addition to the repair of wagons and coaches. With Mr. Richardson's store on one side and his tavern on the other, Mr. Harrington's customers could pass the time in comfort while awaiting the repair of their vehicles.

Soon after the new roads were established, new houses followed suit. Several new homes were built in West Village in the years between 1824 and 1841. The first of these was Thomas B. Gill's Cape Cod–style home at 80 Hubbardston Road. This house was built in 1824 and was later joined by an attached barn and a free-standing blacksmith's shop. This house is thought to have been part of the Underground Railroad, judging by a second-story hiding place concealed by removable shelving. Just west of Thomas Gill's farmstead, William Eveleth built his home around 1841. This 86 Hubbardston Road house is composed of two distinct two-story sections joined by a one-story entry section.

The year 1830 was a busy time for building in West Village. Peter Farrar built his 33 Hubbardston Road home in the fashionable Greek Revival style, with full-length sidelights and an entry porch with corner pilasters. A very similar-looking house stands at 133 Hubbardston Road. Alden Wilder built this house in 1844 on a portion of his grandfather Samuel Woods's farm. Edward Merrick was the next owner and may have added some of the classic Greek Revival features, including the pedimented entry and paneled pilasters.

Sometime before 1830, William Smith built his 28 Radford Road home. While the main part of this house is Greek Revival in style, the rear ell of the house has the look of a Cape Cod cottage and was likely built first. Around the same time, Dr. Alphonso Brooks built his 2 Radford Road home. This house displays its Greek Revival origins in the way of the enclosed façade gable and molded cornice. At around the same time, the house across the street at 52 Hubbardston Road was built in the Federal style, with large double chimneys emerging from a hipped roof. The house at 9 Allen Hill Road was also built around 1830. Old photos show that at one time this house looked just like the houses at 33 and 133 Hubbardston Road. The Greek Revival style remained popular in 1840, when local builder Wilkes Roper built his 12 Radford Road home in his own interpretation of the style.

In the midst of the ongoing residential development, commercial development in West Village increased as well. In 1830, Peter Richardson sold the popular Bullock's Stand to Captain Edward Goodnow. The Goodnow family was operating a tavern and inn at their 113 Goodnow Road home when their attention turned to West Village.

Captain Goodnow continued to operate Bullock's Stand with his sons Erastus and Edward. The building also served as a boardinghouse for people employed in nearby trades and on local farms. The Goodnows expanded their business to include the manufacture and sale of palm leaf hats, boots

Laden with trunks, the Mountain House stage pauses. Just beyond stands the house at 44 Hubbardston Road as it appeared in the nineteenth century. *Princeton Historical Society.*

and shoes. The hand-woven hats were made in Princeton's households on the "putting-out" system, with the Goodnows acting as sales agents. In these early years, Edward A. Goodnow acted as teamster for the family business, rising at two in the morning to drive goods to Boston and return with supplies for the store.

In January 1833, the Goodnow store and tenement building suffered a devastating fire. Three resident families and several boarders stood in subzero temperatures while their home burned before them. Many people suffered frostbite that evening. Goods from the store were destroyed, and two resident mechanics lost their tools to the fire. Furniture, clothing and personal possessions were also destroyed.

The Goodnows immediately rebuilt the store and tenement building. In the process of rebuilding, they expanded their boot and shoe manufacturing with the addition of a two-story wing. Within a few years, the appeal of shoe manufacturing spread. Dr. Alphonso Brooks established a shoe manufactory in the ell of his home at 2 Radford Road. Dr. Brooks was a physician, justice of the peace and, by 1840, a shoemaker as well.

About that time another Goodnow family member settled in West Village. Lois Goodnow, sister of Edward and Erastus, purchased the house at 52

Hubbardston Road with her husband, Colonel Solon Hastings. Colonel Hastings served as a local "squire" who loaned money, drew up contracts and held mortgages. He was also an early member of the Worcester Agricultural Society, a director of the Worcester Mutual Fire Insurance Company and was responsible for the U.S. census for the Princeton area in 1850 and 1870. By 1854, he had accumulated the largest personal estate in Princeton. Hastings represented Princeton and two other towns in the General Court and also served as state senator. In their later years, the Hastingses spent only summers in their West Village home but remained active in town affairs. The Hastingses also played a significant role in the formation of the Princeton Public Library. Lois Hastings was among a group of women who founded the Princeton Ladies' Reading Society, one of several mid-nineteenth-century social libraries in town. For many years, the society's circulating collection was kept in the Hastingses' house. When Mrs. Hastings's brother Edward donated the Goodnow Memorial Building to the town for a public library and school, it was at her suggestion that the Ladies' Reading Society collection (which totaled over one thousand volumes) be donated to the library.

Edward Goodnow left Princeton in 1847 and eventually settled in Worcester. He continued to work in the shoe industry and later became president of the First National Bank. Mr. Goodnow accumulated a considerable fortune and was well known for his philanthropy.

METHODY CORNERS: DIVINE INSPIRATION

West Village was a self-sufficient community in many respects, with its own stores, school, industry and taverns. It seems natural, then, that the residents would establish a place of worship as well. The church they built became the basis of a new identity for West Village

Silas Fay Jr. was the first West Village resident, in 1838, to request dismissal from the Congregational Church in order to join the Methodist Episcopal Church in Worcester. Many of his West Village neighbors followed him, and within a year, Princeton's Methodist Society was formed. Construction of a church quickly followed. By early 1840, the Methodist Church was complete. The church stood at the intersection of Hubbardston, Allen Hill and Radford Roads. Shortly thereafter, the West Village crossroads became known as "Methodist" or "Methody Corners."

Two of the church founders built homes very close to their new church. Jonas Brooks, who owned a farm in the southwest part of town, built a two-

"Methody Corners" in the 1840s, as captured by Princeton artist Rosalind Allen Sturges. *Princeton Historical Society*.

Standing at the corner of Radford and Hubbardston Road is the Methodist Church, cornerstone of the West Village community for over fifty years. *Princeton Historical Society*.

family house next door at 39 Hubbardston Road. Erastus Goodnow built a cottage at 42 Hubbardston Road as a rental house for employees. Later this house was sold to the Methodist Church for use as a parsonage.

The Methodist Church stood at the heart of the village until 1892, when it was struck by lightning. The steeple caught fire and a can of kerosene exploded in the basement. Volunteers rushed to extinguish the fire and managed to save neighboring buildings, but the church itself could not be saved. The Congregational Church members invited the Methodist members to worship with them or use the Congregational Church for their own services. The Methodist Church was not rebuilt.

STAY A WHILE: HOTELS, INNS AND SUMMER HOMES

By the mid-nineteenth century, improved roads and increased stage lines made Princeton's clean air, cool temperatures and scenic vistas accessible to large numbers of summer visitors. The first hotels to cater to this rise in tourism were the Mountain House and the Grand View Hotel on Wachusett Mountain. Princeton gained further popularity as a summer destination when the Boston, Barre & Gardner Railroad began running through town. Several additional hotels were built to accommodate the growing summer population. Stage traffic from Princeton Depot traveled along Hubbardston Road (known at that time as Depot Road) and passed right through West Village, giving the village an opportunity to share in the tourism boom. Several residences in West Village began operating as inns, known at the time as guesthouses or boardinghouses, which served vacationers as well as seasonal employees.

West Village had one hotel of its own. Mount Pleasant House was built between 1857 and 1860 by Charles Whittaker and Rufus Gleason at 34 Goodnow Road. Mr. Whittaker enlarged the building in 1868. The hotel was further enlarged in 1875 to include a third story topped with a mansard roof. In 1879, Whittaker's son-in-law, Moses C. Goodnow, began managing the hotel, which eventually grew to accommodate sixty overnight guests. The hotel included an attached carriage house with a bowling alley. Among Princeton's hotels, Mount Pleasant House was appraised to be of the third highest value.

In 1869, the Grimes family opened the house at 48 Hubbardston Road as an inn called Forest House. Known also as "Grimes Cottage," this inn had fifteen to twenty guest rooms, as well as a kitchen and servants' quarters located in the ell at 2 Allen Hill Road.

An early advertisement promotes the elegance and amenities offered at Mount Pleasant House. *Princeton Historical Society*.

The Pratt family of Worcester played a starring role in the hospitality business in West Village. In 1875, the Pratts purchased the house at the corner of Radford and Hubbardston Roads. This house, at 2 Radford Road, became the first of several West Village inns owned and operated by the Pratt family. Their first inn was called Linden House but soon took the name Pratt's Cottage. The establishment was operated by Mrs. Harriet Pratt and her daughters, Lillian and Harriet. For over three decades, Pratt's Cottage was known for its home cooking and high level of service. Pratt's Cottage underwent some renovations around 1900 to better serve its guests. The right side of the house was extended to accommodate a dining room and an open terrace was added, from which guests could enjoy the view of Wachusett Mountain. The entry porch with Tuscan columns was also added at that time.

In the early 1890s, Mrs. Pratt's son Arthur acquired the house across the street at 52 Hubbardston Road. This house became an inn known as Pratt's Annex and was also managed by Mrs. Pratt and her daughters. At

In 1869, the Grimes family opened their home as an inn named Forest House. Guests enjoyed fresh produce from the Grimeses' nearby farm and orchards. *Princeton Historical Society*.

first, Pratt's Cottage and Pratt's Annex catered only to summer visitors, but eventually both houses remained open year-round.

Around 1890, Herbert A. Pratt built a very large house just south of Pratt's Cottage called Ambleside. Although the building is no longer standing, a massive rubble post that once marked the entrance to the Ambleside property still stands on Radford Road. It is also interesting to note that the newest house old enough to be considered "historical" in West Village was built in 1955 next to the site of Ambleside. This house, built by Henry Smith for Kenneth Vaughan at 8 Radford Road, is of the same Cape Cod cottage style as West Village's earliest house.

In 1892, Mr. Pratt acquired the neighboring house at 12 Radford Road, which he also operated as an inn. This house was first known as Sunnyside Cottage, and by 1895, it took the name Fairside. Herbert Pratt operated Fairside as an inn until 1907. Mr. Pratt's son Brant became the next owner of Fairside. Brant was also responsible for bringing the daily mail from Princeton Depot to the post office located in Pratt's Cottage.

Known for excellent service and cooking, Pratt's Cottage is shown here with its recently expanded dining room and new veranda. A portion of the former Ambleside building appears in the left corner. *Princeton Historical Society.*

This Mediterranean-style villa was the summer residence of Thomas Allen of Boston. Allen established a summer compound with extensive gardens and orchards. *Princeton Historical Society.*

Princeton's thriving tourist industry was a time of prosperity for West Village's farmers as well, who provided meat, butter, cheese, produce and other products to Princeton's hotels and inns. George Mason's farm at 110 Hubbardston Road provided cattle, sheep and pigs for market. Poultry was also raised on the farm, providing both meat and eggs to the hotels and inns. The Grimes family also operated a farm in conjunction with their cottage. In 1870, four hundred pounds of butter were produced on the Grimeses' farm. Both the Masons and the Grimeses maintained apple orchards and small vineyards on their farms as well.

By the late nineteenth century, many of Princeton's longtime summer visitors began to purchase land in Princeton. Some West Village properties became gentlemen's farms or rural retreats for city dwellers from Boston,

Worcester and other New England cities. Owners typically reused existing farm buildings and often employed a resident farmer to work the land through the growing season and look after the estate during the winter. For example, in 1893 Thomas Allen of Boston acquired a large portion of the Fay Farm and built a large Mediterranean-style villa and extensive country estate.

Mr. Allen also acquired the Fays' house at 20 Allen Hill Road, which he updated with plumbing and other amenities. At that time, the Fays' barn was moved across the road to its present location. A house was built nearby for Mr. Allen's farm manager by local builder John C.F. Mirick.

Over the next several years, the Allen property was developed to include tennis courts, orchards, Japanese gardens and a network of carriage roads. Several outbuildings were added as well, including icehouses, a pump house, a greenhouse and a large henhouse. Just outside the entrance to 33 Allen Hill Road stands the former stable and carriage house of the Allen estate. The two main sections were built between 1895 and 1900. The square shape of each section, the shallow hipped roof, deep overhanging eaves and long windows are all features of the Prairie style. The attached garage was a later addition, yet it shares the features of the main building.

One of the unique features of the Allen estate that remains today is the livestock pass beneath Allen Hill Road. This tunnel allowed the Allens' sheep herd to pass safely from barnyard to pasture without crossing the road.

Another country estate was established by John Marcou of Cambridge, who acquired the farm at 73 Hubbardston Road in 1898, followed by the farm at 110 Hubbardston Road in 1907. The house at 73 Hubbardston Road became the home of Marcou's farm manager, who cared for a prizewinning herd of over thirty dairy cows. The 110 Hubbardston Road property (totaling 170 acres) also remained a working farm with four barns, henhouses, a slaughterhouse and a workshop.

Some wealthy city dwellers built new houses during this period. In 1910, Susan Minns of Boston purchased land on Radford Road from John Marcou. It is said that an old publishing house in England was the inspiration for her large stone and wood Shingle-style summer home at 38 Radford Road. Miss Minns's family home was on Louisburg Square in Boston, but like many regular visitors, she ultimately established year-round residency in Princeton.

Following John Marcou's death in 1912, Susan Minns purchased both of his farms. She renovated many of the buildings on those properties and built some new facilities as well. The picturesque stone and concrete swimming pool opposite the farmhouse at 110 Hubbardston Road was one of her additions. Minns's enthusiasm for stone construction is also evidenced by nearby flat-

Thomas Allen Jr. enjoying the view from one of the family's several terraced gardens. *Princeton Historical Society.*

For the safety of his animals, Mr. Allen created this livestock pass beneath Allen Hill Road. *Joyce Anderson.*

topped stone walls and rubble gateposts. Miss Minns appears to have left her mark at the 73 Hubbardston Road house as well, in the way of the stucco siding on both the house and engine house. The stone garage was probably built during that time as well. Minns's estate eventually grew to include Little Wachusett Mountain, a 140-acre parcel just north of the West Village district. A small plaque mounted on a rock on Mountain Road commemorates her donation of Little Wachusett as a state wildlife sanctuary.

THE END OF AN ERA

By the early twentieth century, Princeton's resort industry began to decline. This was undoubtedly due to the advent of the automobile, which provided significantly more flexibility for travelers than the stagecoach and railway. Vacationers were no longer limited to extended stays at one location.

Despite the end of the hotel era, Princeton remained a favorite destination for those who could afford summer properties. Many houses in West Village were purchased and remodeled by wealthy city dwellers as summer homes. The trend set in West Village by Thomas Allen, John Marcou and Susan Minns was followed by many city dwellers on a smaller scale. Several homes were renovated with modern conveniences while their architectural features were carefully retained. Some houses were moved to other locations within West Village.

The former wheelwright shop at 46 Hubbardston Road was purchased by Bostonian Isaac Jackson around 1906. Mr. Jackson turned the house 180 degrees and made the wheelwright's wing into part of the residence. A long arbor was built on the rear part of the property, stretching back to Allen Hill Road.

The most extensively renovated building at this time was Mount Pleasant House. When owner Moses Goodnow and his family moved to the West Coast, they sold the hotel to brothers Harry and Edward Whitney of Worcester. The east half of Mount Pleasant House was moved next door to 26 Goodnow Road, where it was remodeled as a summer home for Edward Whitney and his family. The west half remained on site at 34 Goodnow Road as a residence for Harry Whitney and his wife. Other buildings associated with the hotel were auctioned off and moved to other locations. An ell of the hotel was detached and moved to 90 Hubbardston Road, where it was made into a home for Ben Nelson, the Whitneys' farmer.

Around 1919, the house at 48 Hubbardston Road was acquired by Charlotte Crocker, wife of Alvah Crocker, Fitchburg's largest industrialist.

The Crockers also acquired the Goodnow homestead on Goodnow Road, which they continued to operate as a working farm. In 1957, they donated the farm to the Massachusetts Audubon Society as a wildlife sanctuary. The public has enjoyed Wachusett Meadow as a peaceful oasis ever since.

Shortly after purchasing the house at 48 Hubbardston Road, Mrs. Crocker gave the property to her former minister, Reverend James DeWolf Perry. The reason for this gesture stems from a very personal story. Mrs. Crocker was the godmother of Reverend Perry's daughter, Beatrice, and put money aside for Beatrice's education. Sadly, Beatrice died when she was only six years old. Mrs. Crocker used the money she had put aside to purchase the house, which she then gave to Reverend Perry.

Perry spent summers at the house with his family through the 1950s. Perry's wife, Edith, was the daughter of artist John Ferguson Weir, first dean of the School of Fine Arts at Yale University. One year when Edith's father visited the house, the two of them sketched scenes of the house as they imagined it in earlier years. These images are still in place on the dining room wall.

Luke Griffin acquired his family's 9 Allen Hill Road house as his summer home early in the twentieth century. Mr. Griffin is said to have made a fortune dealing in real estate in Worcester and Holyoke. He eventually lived in Princeton year-round.

Another trend in West Village around the early part of the twentieth century was the acquisition of smaller properties by Princeton's wealthy summer residents for their employees, relatives or associates. Mrs. Charles Washburn of 30 Mountain Road bought the house at 33 Hubbardston Road to rent to employees of her husband's Worcester-based business, the Washburn Wire Company. Henry C. Delano of 58 Mountain Road bought the old schoolhouse at 36 Hubbardston Road for his employees Michael and Mary Kivlon.

There was also new construction of year-round residences in West Village during that period. In 1901, Samuel Shapleigh of Boston had a stone cottage built as a summer residence at 14 Goodnow Road. That house burned in 1930 but is not forgotten. In 1945, Sandy Harpell, an active builder in Princeton in the 1940s and '50s, built a house at 14 Goodnow Road using much of the stone from Mr. Shapleigh's cottage. Mr. Shapleigh also owned the large Italianate-style house at 4 Goodnow Road, built in 1878 by Edward Merrick.

In 1902, local builder Remington Hamilton built his Colonial Revival–style house (known as an American Four Square) at 12 Allen Hill Road, where he lived year-round. Mr. Hamilton is also known for building the

Princeton Center School on Boylston Avenue and for constructing the Aladdin "kit" house for Thomas Allen Jr. at 32 Allen Hill Road. Both of these buildings are located just outside West Village in the Princeton Center Historic District.

In 1903, Mary Houghton had a Colonial Revival–style house built where the Methodist Church stood, at 43 Hubbardston Road. She later sold the house to her daughter Harriett E.B. Houghton, who was a well-known Princeton schoolteacher.

The large Shingle-style house at 13 Goodnow Road was built around 1909 as a summer house for Mr. and Mrs. George McIntire. Typical of Shingle-style houses is the combined use of wood and stone, which can be found on both the nearby garage and well house.

LOCAL BUILDERS

Some of the houses in West Village are particularly notable for their connections to local builders who contributed much to Princeton's development.

While living at his 12 Radford Road home, Remington Hamilton built a large barn a short distance away for use as a combined workshop, sawmill and lumber storage shed for the construction business he shared with his partner, Frederick Bryant. He later built a house next door to his workshop at 7 Radford Road—a Colonial Revival–style home with features drawn from the Queen Anne, Shingle and Greek Revival styles.

Mr. Hamilton completed the house in 1909 and moved in with his wife, Bella, and children, eight-year-old Beatrice and three-year-old Richmond. Richmond eventually followed in his father's footsteps. In 1928, he built the only Craftsman-style bungalow in West Village at 11 Radford Road, where he lived with his wife. With the addition of Richmond's house, together with Remington's house, sawmill and workshop next door at 7 Radford Road, a small company compound was formed.

In 1930, Remington Hamilton purchased the building at 35–37 Hubbardston Road. It was built around 1888 by Henry Howard and became the West Village Meat Market in 1898. Mr. Hamilton installed a gas pump for automobile travelers and rented the upstairs apartment to his employees. Remington and Richmond Hamilton became business partners in 1936. That year they built a gas station and automobile repair shop at 23 Hubbardston Road, which included an office and space for lumber storage. For nearly thirty years, R.H. Hamilton & Son maintained its office in this building.

Like the coaches they replaced, the early automobiles passing through West Village needed servicing of their own. Hamilton's Garage met that need. *Princeton Historical Society.*

Remington and Richmond Hamilton established a regional reputation as builders of both new construction and restoration. Among their later projects were the Christadelphian Church in Ware and the restoration of the Petersham Town Hall. The Hamiltons' best-known local work includes the restoration of the Boylston farmhouse on Worcester Road. They also acted as caretakers for many of the summer houses in Princeton, including the Reverend DeWolf Perry's summer home. Like the Pratt family before them, the Hamiltons operated a successful family business at the heart of West Village for decades.

West Village has evolved from a farming community to a busy commercial center to a quiet residential neighborhood. Farming continues at the Smith Farm at 110 Hubbardston Road, mainly in the form of haying. Some commerce remains at the former Hamilton Garage, which is now home to the Princeton House of Pizza.

Numerous old barns, open fields and stone walls make it easy to envision West Village's agricultural past. Much less obvious is the nearly one hundred years of bustling activity that followed. The houses of West Village have played many roles throughout its long history, serving as residences, schools, taverns, inns, shops and even factories. Recognizing these houses and their contribution to Princeton's development will help keep the history of West Village alive.

THE TRUTH ABOUT NATIONAL REGISTER HISTORIC DISTRICTS

There are a lot of misconceptions floating around about the National Register of Historic Places. We can blame that on an unfortunate accident of language. "Local Historic District" and "National Register Historic District" are easy to confuse, but they are very different.

When a district is included on the National Register of Historic Places, property owners' rights are not changed in any way. Local zoning laws do not change. Inclusion in the National Register is an honor, acknowledging the significance of these properties to all citizens of the United States.

The National Register is a program of the National Park Service. It is America's official listing of sites important to the story of American history. The National Register includes national landmarks, as designated by the secretary of the interior, and significant properties and areas nominated by local historical commissions and then approved by the National Park Service.

The bar is set high for approval. To be considered, properties must be associated with important historical events or individuals, embody a distinctive kind of architecture or yield important historical information. For a district to qualify, it must include a significant number of properties that qualify as historic. Newer properties within the boundaries of a historic district are considered "noncontributing" if they are less than fifty years old at the time of nomination.

Individual buildings or structures may be listed in the National Register. In the case of Princeton, four distinct districts have met the criteria for listing.

To place a district on the National Register, a local historical commission applies to the Massachusetts Historical Commission. The first step is to prepare a comprehensive local inventory of all of a district's features that contribute to its qualification. Inventories capture basic information about the historic, architectural and archaeological significance of individual properties, as well as the district as a whole. The Massachusetts Historical Commission reviews the inventory to decide if it is worthy of listing in the National Register. The final approval and determination rests with the National Park Service.

The Princeton Historical Commission has, to date, succeeded in placing three districts (Princeton Center, East Princeton and Russell Corner) and one building (Fernside) on the National Register. West Village has been nominated for inclusion. There are many structures in Princeton that may meet the requirements for inclusion in the National Register that have not yet been nominated. This book celebrates most, but not all, of the buildings within the districts that have been so far honored.

ARCHITECTURAL DEFINITIONS

balustrade: a railing composed of posts (balusters) and a handrail; example, 7 Hubbardston Road porch roof.

bays: the number of openings (doors and windows) on the ground floor of a building.

bay window: a large window or series of windows projecting from the outer wall of a building and forming a recess within; example, 10 Mountain Road.

bracket: any horizontal projecting support for an overhanging weight; example, 19 Merriam Road.

Cape Cod: originated in New England in the seventeenth century; it is traditionally characterized by a low, broad frame building, generally a story and a half high with end gables and a large central chimney.

cistern: a receptacle for holding liquid, especially a tank for catching and storing rainwater.

Colonial Revival: a late nineteenth-century American style movement harkening back to colonial-era architecture; example, 5 Hubbardston Road.

Corinthian capital: the top portion of a column shaped like an inverted bell, decorated with acanthus leaves; example, 66 Main Street.

Appendix B

cornice: the uppermost section of molding(s) along the top of a wall or just below a roof; examples, a simple boxed cornice appears at 42 Hubbardston Road, while a more elaborate, bracketed cornice appears at 26 Goodnow Road.

cupola: a light structure on a dome or roof, serving as a belfry or lantern; examples, barn at 66 Main Street and house at 19 Merriam Road.

dentils: a series of small rectangular blocks projecting like teeth from a molding or beneath a cornice.

dormer: a gabled extension built out from a sloping roof to accommodate a vertical window; example, the ell on 48 Hubbardston Road.

dry-laid stone: stone structures built without mortar.

Dutch Colonial: an American architectural style characterized by a gambrel (curved eave) roof; example, 20 Mountain Road.

eaves: the edge of a roof; they usually project beyond the side of the building generally to provide weather protection.

entablature: the part of a classical building supported by the columns, consisting of an architrave (molding), a frieze and a cornice.

eyebrow dormer: a dormer with a bell curve shape on top and a straight horizontal bottom, resembling an eyebrow example, 38 Radford Road.

façade: generally one side of the exterior of a building, "typically" the front; the word comes from the French language, literally meaning "frontage" or "face."

fanlight: a semicircular window over a door or another window; example, front door at 20 Allen Hill Road.

Federal: the period pertaining to, or designating, the style of architecture current in the United States from around 1780 to 1840; it is lighter and more symmetrical than Georgian and reflects the ideals of the new United States; example, 49 Gregory Hill Road.

fenestration: the design and disposition of windows and other exterior openings of a building.

frieze: a decorative band at the top or beneath a cornice.

gable: the portion of the front or side of a building enclosed by a pitched roof.

gable-ended: an end wall bearing a gable.

Georgian: a style of architecture popular in America from 1700 to 1830 and referring to the reign of King George; identifying features are double-hung windows, paneled doors, cornices with dentils and windows symmetrically balanced; example, 16 Merriam Road, 28 Merriam Road.

Greek Revival: a style of architecture prevalent in the United States in the first half of the nineteenth century, most often characterized by a gable-end façade, pilasters and columns, imitating ancient Greek designs; examples, Mechanics Hall, First Congregational Church, 15 Gregory Hill Road.

hip roof: a type of roof where all sides slope downward to the walls, usually with a fairly gentle slope and no gables; example, 12 Allen Hill Road.

Italianate: a popular Victorian architectural style that was inspired by the Italian Renaissance of the fifteenth and sixteenth centuries.

mansard roof: a dual pitched hip roof, often with dormer windows on the steep lower slope; example, 6 Mountain Road.

oculus window: a round window that appears eyelike; example, First Congregational Church.

pediment: a wide, low-pitched gable above the façade of a building in the Grecian style.

pilaster: a rectangular support that resembles a flat column; the pilaster projects only slightly from the wall and has a base, a shaft and a capital; example, 48 Hubbardston Road.

portico: a porch or generally a covered walkway with a roof supported by columns, often leading to the entrance of a building.

Queen Anne: a dominant style of American architecture in the late nineteenth century that revived the style of English decorative arts during the reign of Queen Anne (1702–1714); example, 11 Prospect Street.

Richardsonian Romanesque: a late nineteenth-century style of architecture named afte architect Henry Hobson Richardson, frequently referred to as Romanesque; example, Princeton Public Library.

Romanesque: a revival style that emphasizes clear, strong, picturesque massing, round-headed arches often springing from clusters of short squat columns, recessed entrances and turrets; example, Bagg Hall.

shed dormer: a dormer window whose eave line is parallel to the eave line of the main roof.

Shingle: a style of wood, shingle-covered American architecture popular in the Victorian era; identifying features are walls and roofing of continuous wood shingles and extensive porches; examples, 38 Radford Road, 13 Goodnow Road.

sidelights: a narrow, vertical section of windows on either side of a door that spans the full or partial length of the door; examples, 14 and 15 Gregory Hill Road.

spindle balustrade: a balustrade made with narrow, decorative shafts of wood.

Stick: a style in mid-Victorian American architecture; example, former chapel at 81 Main Street. (The chapel has alternating sections of shingle and clapboard siding, a picket fence pattern along the eaves and diagonal stick work in the bell tower.)

transom: a window above a door but within the vertical frame of the door; example, 49 Gregory Hill Road.

turret: a small tower or tower-shaped projection on a building; example, Bagg Hall (town hall).

Tuscan: a style of classical architecture from the Tuscany regions of Italy, characterized by unfluted columns; example, 7 Hubbardston Road.

veranda: a porch or balcony, usually roofed and often partly enclosed, extending along the outside of a building; example, 30 Mountain Road and 4 Goodnow Road.

Vernacular: a style of architecture exemplifying the commonest techniques, decorative features and materials of a particular historical period, region or group of people.

BIBLIOGRAPHY

PUBLICATIONS

Anderson, Joyce Bailey. *Princeton and Wachusett Mountain*. Charleston, SC: Arcadia Publishing, 2003.

Baumgardner, George H. *Princeton and the High Road 1775–1975*. Princeton, MA: Bicentennial Commission, 1975.

Blake, Francis Everett. *History of the Town of Princeton 1759–1915*. Vol. 1, *Narratives*, and Vol. 2, *Genealogies*. Princeton, MA: Town of Princeton, 1915.

Dahl, Curtis. *Stephen C. Earle, Architect: Shaping Worcester's Image*. Worcester, MA: Worcester Historical Museum, 1980s.

Galluzzo, John J. *Mass Audubon*. Charleston, SC: Arcadia Publishing, 2005.

Gilbert, Paul T., comp. *Princeton, Mass., Illustrated*. Gardner, MA: Gardner News Co., 1900. Reprint, 1972.

Hanaford, Jeremiah Lyford. *History of Princeton, Worcester County, Massachusetts: Civil and Ecclesiastical, From Its First Settlement in 1739 to April 1852*. Worcester, MA: C. Buckingham Webb, 1852.

Hurd, D.H. *History of Worcester County, Mass*. Philadelphia: J.W. Lewis & Co., 1889.

Princeton, Mass. 1759–1959: The Princeton Story. 200th Anniversary of the Town of Princeton. Princeton Historical Society, 1959.

Russell, Charles T. *History of Princeton, Worcester County, Massachusetts*. Boston: Henry P. Lewis, 1838.

Whitney, Peter. *History of the County of Worcester in the Commonwealth of Massachusetts*. Worcester, MA: Isaiah Thomas, 1793.

BIBLIOGRAPHY

DEEDS

Title searches were performed on the following properties in the four National Historic Register Districts: 20 Allen Hill Road; 7 Boylston Avenue; 4 Goodnow Road; 5 Prospect Street; 8 and 12 Radford Road; 11, 13 and 15 Gregory Hill Road; 19, 42, 44, 48, 80, 133 and 136 Hubbardston Road; 70, 76, 77 and 80 Main Street; 6 and 8 Merriam Road; and 6 and 10 Mountain Road.

PRINCETON HISTORICAL SOCIETY COLLECTION

Allen, Eleanor. "Recollections of Seventy Summers in Princeton." Ca. 1960.

Beaman, Harry C. "Princeton Town Halls." October 11, 1943.

"The Corne Mill." N.d.

Davis, Abby Wilder. "Notes and Anecdotes of Old Princeton." Presented by her daughter, Florence Marguerite Davis, October 6, 1942.

Gregory, Josiah D. "Princeton Post Offices." 1915.

———. "A Talk on Princeton's Early Settlers." 1920.

Houghton, Mrs. Herbert, and Mrs. Kenneth Whelan. "Princeton Schools." 1942.

Lapoint, Carl. "Some Princeton Businesses, A History." January 1969.

———. "A Tour of Princeton's Mill Sites." June 9, 1999.

Llewellyn, Eleanor S. "Princeton's First Two Hundred Years." Typewritten paper for the Bay State Historical League, October 6, 1960.

Mirick, Ethel R. "A Short History of the Third Meeting House, 1838–1938." N.d.

Morgan, Philip. "The Boston, Barre, and Gardner Railroad." 1956.

Peck, Reverend Charles Russell. "Charles Russell." 1966.

Poor, Katherine. "Remarks Prepared and Delivered by Katherine Poor on the Occasion of a Bus Tour of Princeton, Massachusetts on August 11, 1968." Unpublished typescript, 1968.

"Princeton Bands." N.d.

Princeton Historical Society documents, photographs, research and scrapbook files.

Roper, Mary. "Land Utilization of the Town of Princeton." March 1944.

Traver, Brad. Untitled paper about Princeton schools. May 1979.

Woodward, Anita, and Clayton Hubbard. "Princeton House File." Ca. 1972.

NEWSPAPER ARTICLES

Booth, Phyllis. "Bells, Books & Candles: A Reflection on Princeton Schools." *Landmark*, July 6, 2000.

———. "Growing Up in East Princeton." *Landmark*, July 16, 1998.

———. "Hotels Flourished, Then Perished." *Landmark*, July 7, 1994.

———. "In Retrospect: Recalling Princeton's Past." *Landmark*, July 21, 1988.

———. "Old Princeton Mills and Factories." *Landmark*, July 19, 1990.

———. "Plane Spotters in Princeton." *Landmark*, July 6, 1995.

———. "A Scrapbook of Princeton History: Looking Back at Princeton's Schools." *Landmark*, July 18, 1991.

"Mechanics Hall." *Telegram and Gazette*, January 22, 1978.

"Princeton Chapel." *Telegram and Gazette*, November 14, 1945, and June 25, 1960.

MASSACHUSETTS GOVERNMENT DOCUMENTS

Anderson, Joyce, et al. *Survey and Inventory of Historic, Architectural, and Cultural Resources of Princeton*. Boston: Massachusetts Historical Commission, n.d.

Cavanaugh, Katharine. Princeton Center National Register Historic District Boundary Expansion Nomination. Accepted December 14, 2005. Massachusetts Historical Commission, Boston.

———. Russell Corner National Register Historic District Nomination. Accepted December 14, 2005. Massachusetts Historical Commission, Boston.

Ceccacci, Susan. East Princeton Village National Register Historic District Nomination. Accepted March 18, 2004. Massachusetts Historical Commission, Boston.

———. Princeton Center National Register Historic District Nomination. Accepted April 1999. Massachusetts Historical Commission, Boston.

Forbes, Anne. West Village National Register Historic District Nomination. Submitted to Massachusetts Historical Commission, July 2, 2007. Massachusetts Historical Commission, Boston.

Historic and Archaeological Resources of Central Massachusetts. Boston: Massachusetts Historical Commission, 1985.

Massachusetts Heritage Landscape Inventory Program. *Princeton Reconnaissance Report*. Boston: Massachusetts Department of Conservation and Recreation and Freedom's Way Heritage Association, 2006.

BIBLIOGRAPHY

Reconnaissance Survey Report for Princeton. Boston: Massachusetts Historical Commission, 1984.

TOWN OF PRINCETON DOCUMENTS

Annual Reports: School Department Reports. 1876, 1885 and 1892.
Annual Reports of the Town of Princeton. Various dates.
Assessor's Computer Assisted Massachusetts Appraisal System
Historic House Plaque Reports. Princeton Historical Commission, 2006–2008.
Tax Ledgers, Tax Valuations and Assessors Records. 1767 to present.
Vital Records of Princeton, Massachusetts to the End of the Year 1849. Worcester, MA: Franklin P. Rice, 1902.
Vital Records of the Town of Princeton

INTERVIEWS

Anderson, Joyce. Chair, Princeton Historical Commission, 2005.
Bingham, Marjorie. "Personal Recollections of East Princeton," March 1997.
Bullock, Bunny. Princeton resident, 2005.
Cary, Deborah. Princeton resident, 2008.
Chute, Judith. Great-granddaughter of Augustus G. Bullock, 2005.
Hubbard, Arthur. "Personal Recollections of East Princeton," March 1997.
Hubbard, Edith. "Personal Recollections of East Princeton," March 1997.
Mason, Anne. Princeton resident, November 2008.
Slongwhite, Donald, and Carolyn Slongwhite. "Personal Recollections of East Princeton," March 2002.

MAPS AND ATLASES

Allen, Rosalind Sturges. *The Illustrated Map Celebrating the Fiftieth Anniversary of the Princeton Historical Society.* Princeton, MA: Princeton Historical Society, 1987.
———. *Map of West Village.* 1997.
Assessor's Maps. Town of Princeton, 1998.
Atlas of Worcester County. New York: F.W. Beers, 1870.
Carter, James. *Map of Worcester County.* 1845 and 1855.

Merriam, Amos. *Plan of Princeton, Massachusetts*. October 1830. With early divisions and province grants plotted by Francis Blake, 1911. Delineated by K.A. Mossman.

Murphy, Marion. "Princeton Houses Built Before 1859." Prepared for the 200th anniversary of the town of Princeton, Massachusetts, 1959.

New Topographical Atlas of Worcester County. Philadelphia: Beers, Richards, L.J., 1898.

Walling, Henry. *Map of Worcester County, Massachusetts*. Boston: William Baker, 1857.

ABOUT THE AUTHORS

Joyce Anderson, Alexandra Fiandaca and Sheila Dubman are all members of the Princeton Historical Commission.

Joyce Anderson, chair of the commission, has been a resident of Princeton since 1981 and chair since 1997. In this capacity, she has worked to catalogue and recognize Princeton's historical buildings and homes. This is the second book that Joyce has written about Princeton (she is the author of *Princeton and Wachusett Mountain*, Images of America, 2005).

Alexandra Fiandaca, vice chair, and Sheila Dubman are more recent transplants to Princeton. Alex was educated as a scientist and spent fourteen years in the biotechnical industry. Sheila has had a thirty-year career in educational consulting and software marketing.

The authors are deeply gratified to have had an opportunity to delve so deeply into Princeton's history. Alexandra's research talent and Sheila's editorial skills were enthusiastic additions to Joyce's leadership in this endeavor. Commitment to the town of Princeton is not unusual, but an opportunity to serve with such a dedicated group is rare.

Visit us at
www.historypress.net